Food Security and Sustainable Development: Advancing Global Food Systems by Integrating Climate Change, Nutrition, Agriculture, Governance, and Trade Solutions

Copyright

Food Security and Sustainable Development: Advancing Global Food Systems by Integrating Climate Change, Nutrition, Agriculture, Governance, and Trade Solutions

© 2025 Robert C. Brears

ISBN (eBook): 978-1-991368-45-4

ISBN (Paperback): 978-1-991368-46-1

Published by Global Climate Solutions

First Edition, 2025

Cover design and interior layout by Global Climate Solutions

Table of Contents

Introduction

Food security sits at the core of sustainable development, linking human well-being with environmental integrity and economic stability. It encompasses the availability, accessibility, utilization, and stability of food supplies that meet dietary needs and preferences for an active and healthy life. The Sustainable Development Goals (SDGs) frame global ambitions to end hunger, achieve food security, improve nutrition, and promote sustainable agriculture. However, the challenge extends beyond SDG 2, as food security connects directly to goals on poverty eradication, health, water, energy, climate, and ecosystems.

The modern food system is complex, involving production, distribution, trade, and consumption patterns that shape economies and societies. While globalization has increased access to diverse foods, it has also heightened vulnerabilities to market fluctuations, supply chain disruptions, and environmental degradation. Climate change threatens agricultural productivity, particularly in regions reliant on rain-fed farming, while biodiversity loss and soil degradation reduce the resilience of ecosystems that underpin global food supplies. Water scarcity and pollution further constrain agricultural systems, especially in arid and semi-arid regions.

At the same time, inequality persists in access to food. Economic disparities, gender inequities, and geographic isolation limit opportunities for millions of people to secure nutritious diets. The rise of urbanization and changing consumption patterns also place additional pressures on natural resources and create a growing need for sustainable production and consumption models. Policies that address both the supply and demand sides of food security are therefore essential to balance economic growth with environmental limits.

Achieving food security in alignment with the SDGs requires systemic transformation. Governments, private sectors, and communities must coordinate efforts to build resilience across food systems, strengthen governance frameworks, and promote equitable access to resources. Technology and innovation offer opportunities to enhance efficiency, transparency, and sustainability, yet these must be guided by ethical principles and inclusive governance.

Food security is a multidimensional issue that calls for collaboration across disciplines and borders. It demands recognition of the interdependence between human and natural systems, where decisions in one sector can affect outcomes in another. By aligning global food systems with the SDGs, it becomes possible to create a future where all people have reliable access to nutritious food produced within the planet's ecological boundaries.

Chapter 1: Understanding Food Security in the Context of Sustainable Development

Food security lies at the core of sustainable development, connecting human well-being with environmental integrity and economic stability. It encompasses the availability, accessibility, utilization, and stability of food systems that ensure all people can obtain sufficient, safe, and nutritious food. Understanding food security within the broader sustainable development context highlights the interdependence of social equity, environmental stewardship, and economic growth.

The Sustainable Development Goals (SDGs) position food security as both a foundational objective and a cross-cutting theme influencing multiple goals, including poverty reduction, health, gender equality, and climate action. Food systems are central to achieving these objectives because they determine how resources are used, how livelihoods are sustained, and how resilience is built in the face of global change.

This chapter explores the evolution, dimensions, and drivers of food security, emphasizing its integration with the SDGs and the transformative approaches required to achieve equitable and sustainable outcomes globally.

Defining Food Security and Its Dimensions

Food security refers to a state in which all individuals, at all times, have physical, social, and economic access to sufficient, safe, and nutritious food that meets their dietary needs and preferences for an active and healthy life. It embodies a comprehensive understanding of the interactions among food availability, access, utilization, and stability, as outlined by the Food and Agriculture Organization of the United Nations. This concept extends beyond simple food supply, encompassing the social, environmental, and economic systems that determine how food is produced, distributed, and consumed.

The first dimension, food availability, concerns the physical presence of food in a country, region, or community. It reflects agricultural production, food imports, stock levels, and distribution mechanisms. Availability depends on multiple factors, including climatic conditions, access to arable land, technological capacity, and trade policies. High yields alone do not guarantee food security if infrastructure, logistics, or governance barriers prevent food from reaching populations in need. The balance between domestic production and imports also influences national resilience to global market volatility and supply disruptions.

The second dimension, food access, refers to the ability of individuals and households to obtain food through purchase, barter, or self-production. Economic access is strongly influenced by income levels, employment opportunities, and market prices. Social access involves the fairness and inclusiveness of food distribution systems, where marginalized groups may face barriers due to discrimination, conflict, or geographic isolation. Even in food-surplus regions, unequal access can persist, resulting in hunger and malnutrition among vulnerable populations.

Food utilization, the third dimension, focuses on how food is used by the body to maintain health and well-being. It encompasses dietary quality, nutritional diversity, and food safety. Proper utilization depends on access to clean water, sanitation, healthcare, and knowledge of nutrition. Inadequate diets and poor health conditions can lead to undernutrition, micronutrient deficiencies, and obesity. The nutritional transition observed in many developing countries highlights a paradox of simultaneous undernutrition and overnutrition, emphasizing the need to integrate food and health policies.

The fourth dimension, stability, captures the temporal aspect of food security. It measures whether availability, access, and utilization are consistent over time or subject to disruption. Stability can be affected by economic shocks, natural disasters, conflicts, or pandemics. Seasonal fluctuations in production and prices also influence stability, particularly in rural and low-income communities. Policies aimed at improving stability include establishing food reserves, diversifying livelihoods, and developing early warning systems to anticipate and mitigate crises.

Food security is shaped by interrelated social, economic, and environmental factors. Urbanization, globalization, demographic shifts, and climate change influence each dimension, requiring adaptive governance and integrated strategies. The multidimensional nature of food security underscores its importance as both a development goal and a policy framework guiding international cooperation and sustainable resource management.

Evolution of Global Food Security Frameworks

The concept of food security has evolved significantly over the past seven decades, reflecting changes in global priorities, governance structures, and understanding of the drivers of hunger and malnutrition. Early discussions in the mid-twentieth century primarily focused on food availability and national self-sufficiency, emphasizing the need to increase agricultural production after periods of conflict and food shortages. This production-centered view dominated the global agenda for decades, shaping policies that prioritized yield growth, industrial farming, and international trade as the main means of addressing hunger.

During the 1970s, a series of food crises drew attention to the limitations of production-focused approaches. The 1974 World Food Conference marked a turning point by broadening the concept of food security to include access and distribution. Governments recognized that global food sufficiency did not necessarily translate into individual or household food security. The conference led to the establishment of new international institutions and mechanisms such as the World Food Council and the International Fund for Agricultural Development to strengthen coordination in addressing hunger and rural poverty.

By the 1980s, research and policy discourse began to emphasize the socioeconomic dimensions of food insecurity. Amartya Sen's entitlement theory played a central role in shifting the focus toward people's ability to access food rather than the quantity of food available. This perspective underscored the importance of income, employment, and social equity in determining food security outcomes. Institutions began to consider poverty reduction, gender equality, and social protection as integral to food policy, expanding the agenda beyond agriculture alone.

In the 1990s, the concept further evolved toward a rights-based framework. The 1996 World Food Summit articulated food security as a universal human right and called for collective global action to halve the number of undernourished people by 2015. This period also saw the emergence of the Millennium Development Goals (MDGs), which linked hunger reduction to broader development objectives such as poverty alleviation, health, and education. International efforts increasingly emphasized partnerships between governments, international organizations, and civil society to improve food access and resilience.

The launch of the Sustainable Development Goals in 2015 represented another major milestone, embedding food security within a comprehensive agenda that integrates social, environmental, and economic dimensions of sustainability. SDG 2, Zero Hunger, established targets not only to end hunger but also to promote sustainable agriculture, improve nutrition, and enhance food system resilience. This holistic approach acknowledges that food security cannot be achieved in isolation from climate action, biodiversity conservation, water management, and responsible consumption.

In recent years, global food security frameworks have continued to evolve to address emerging challenges such as climate change, pandemics, and geopolitical tensions affecting supply chains. The focus has shifted toward building resilient, inclusive, and sustainable food systems that ensure equitable access and environmental stewardship. The growing recognition of interlinkages among the

SDGs reinforces the need for integrated governance mechanisms and cross-sectoral collaboration to strengthen food security at all levels.

Interlinkages Between Food Security and the SDGs

Food security is deeply interwoven with the Sustainable Development Goals, reflecting the multidimensional nature of hunger, nutrition, and sustainable agriculture. While SDG 2 focuses directly on achieving zero hunger, its success depends on progress across numerous other goals that influence or are influenced by the global food system. These interconnections emphasize the need for integrated approaches that consider social, economic, and environmental factors shaping food availability, access, and stability.

The relationship between food security and poverty eradication, outlined in SDG 1, is foundational. Poverty limits the ability of households to purchase or produce adequate food, while food insecurity perpetuates cycles of deprivation by undermining health, productivity, and education outcomes. Improving livelihoods through social protection, income diversification, and rural development contributes directly to reducing hunger and promoting resilience. Economic inclusion and equitable access to resources remain central to breaking the link between hunger and poverty.

SDG 3 on good health and well-being intersects strongly with food security through the dimension of nutrition. Undernutrition, micronutrient deficiencies, and obesity collectively represent the global burden of malnutrition. Ensuring dietary diversity and food safety supports health outcomes by reducing disease and mortality rates, particularly among children and women. Integrating nutrition-sensitive interventions within agricultural and food policies helps align health and food system objectives.

Clean water and sanitation, covered under SDG 6, are essential for the safe production, processing, and consumption of food. Contaminated water sources compromise food safety, increase disease transmission, and limit crop and livestock productivity.

Water scarcity and poor water management reduce agricultural yields and threaten the sustainability of irrigated systems. Efficient water use, wastewater treatment, and sustainable irrigation practices are critical to maintaining both food production and ecosystem integrity.

SDG 7 on affordable and clean energy links to food security through the energy required for agricultural production, transport, storage, and processing. Energy access enables mechanization, irrigation, and cold chain systems, enhancing productivity and reducing post-harvest losses. Transitioning to renewable energy in the food system supports climate mitigation goals while ensuring stable energy supplies for rural communities dependent on agriculture.

Sustainable economic growth and decent work, as addressed in SDG 8, contribute to food security by creating employment opportunities in agriculture, fisheries, and food-related industries. Promoting value-added activities, smallholder entrepreneurship, and fair labor practices strengthens local economies and food supply chains. Policies fostering inclusive economic participation empower rural populations and enhance their capacity to manage risks and adapt to changing conditions.

SDG 12, which focuses on responsible consumption and production, directly influences food security through sustainable supply chains and waste reduction. Around one-third of global food production is lost or wasted each year, representing a major inefficiency in the food system. Encouraging sustainable consumption patterns, improving storage infrastructure, and reducing waste contribute to resource efficiency and equitable food distribution.

Climate action under SDG 13 is central to ensuring long-term food security. Changes in temperature, rainfall, and extreme weather events disrupt agricultural systems, affecting yields and food prices. Adaptation and mitigation strategies, including climate-resilient crops and low-emission farming, support sustainable food production. Integrating food security objectives into climate policies ensures coherence across global development efforts.

Biodiversity and ecosystem conservation, emphasized in SDG 15, underpin food production through pollination, soil fertility, and genetic diversity. The degradation of forests, grasslands, and marine ecosystems reduces the capacity of natural systems to support agriculture. Restoring ecosystems and adopting sustainable land management practices protect these essential services, maintaining the foundation of food systems.

Strong institutions, inclusive governance, and global partnerships outlined in SDGs 16 and 17 provide the enabling environment for achieving food security. Transparent governance, policy coherence, and international cooperation enhance resource mobilization, technology transfer, and data sharing. Coordinated action among governments, private sectors, and civil society ensures that progress on food security aligns with broader sustainable development goals.

Cross-Sectoral Nature of Food Systems

Food systems operate across multiple sectors, linking agriculture, environment, health, trade, and governance. Each of these sectors contributes to and is influenced by how food is produced, processed, distributed, and consumed. The cross-sectoral nature of food systems highlights the need for coordination between policies that affect land, water, energy, and labor to ensure sustainable and equitable outcomes. Fragmented decision-making can create inefficiencies, increase vulnerabilities, and undermine food security objectives.

Agriculture lies at the center of food systems, but its sustainability depends on policies in water, energy, and environmental management. Water availability influences crop yields, while energy access affects irrigation, storage, and processing. Environmental policies determine land-use practices and biodiversity protection, which in turn shape agricultural productivity. Effective integration of these sectors is essential to prevent resource conflicts and promote efficiency in production systems.

Health and nutrition sectors intersect with food systems through their influence on dietary patterns and food utilization. Public health strategies addressing malnutrition, foodborne diseases, and diet-related conditions depend on agricultural and food policies that prioritize nutritional value as well as yield. Education and awareness programs that link food choices with health outcomes help reinforce this connection.

Economic and trade sectors shape access to food through markets, employment, and pricing mechanisms. International trade policies affect the flow of agricultural goods, influencing both producers and consumers. Investments in infrastructure and logistics facilitate market access and reduce post-harvest losses, improving availability and affordability. Fiscal and social protection policies ensure that vulnerable populations can access food even during economic shocks.

Governance and institutional frameworks provide the mechanisms for policy coordination across sectors. Coherent governance structures encourage collaboration among ministries and agencies responsible for agriculture, health, environment, and finance. Multilevel governance linking national, regional, and local actors ensures that strategies are adapted to specific contexts and communities. Transparent data systems and shared accountability mechanisms further strengthen cross-sectoral coordination.

Food systems also intersect with cultural and social dimensions that influence food preferences, consumption habits, and traditional practices. These dimensions affect demand, resource use, and environmental impacts. Understanding such interconnections supports inclusive food system transformation that respects cultural diversity and community knowledge. Cross-sectoral integration is therefore an organizing principle for achieving sustainable, resilient, and equitable food systems aligned with long-term development objectives.

Key Global Challenges to Achieving Food Security

Food security faces a complex array of global challenges driven by interconnected environmental, economic, social, and political factors. Population growth continues to increase demand for food, putting pressure on finite land, water, and energy resources. Expanding urban areas reduce the availability of arable land and alter consumption patterns toward more resource-intensive diets. These shifts heighten the strain on production systems and natural ecosystems, requiring new approaches to manage competing land uses and maintain ecological balance.

Climate change poses one of the most significant threats to food security. Rising temperatures, changing precipitation patterns, and extreme weather events disrupt agricultural productivity and supply chains. Droughts, floods, and heat stress reduce crop yields, degrade soil quality, and increase the vulnerability of smallholder farmers. The frequency of climate-related disasters also undermines food stability by affecting prices and accessibility in global markets. Adaptation and resilience-building efforts are essential to mitigate these risks and maintain stable food systems.

Resource scarcity and degradation further challenge food production. Water scarcity limits irrigation potential in many regions, while pollution from fertilizers and industrial activities affects both water quality and biodiversity. Soil erosion, salinization, and nutrient depletion diminish agricultural capacity and threaten long-term productivity. Unsustainable resource use in agriculture intensifies these pressures, creating feedback loops that weaken resilience to environmental change.

Economic volatility and market dependency also affect global food security. Price fluctuations in international markets, trade restrictions, and supply chain disruptions can quickly translate into

15

food shortages or unaffordable prices for low-income populations. The concentration of production and distribution in a few global actors creates systemic vulnerabilities, especially in developing countries reliant on imports. Economic inequality amplifies disparities in food access, leaving marginalized groups most exposed to food insecurity.

Conflict and political instability remain persistent drivers of hunger. Armed conflicts disrupt agricultural activities, displace populations, and destroy infrastructure necessary for food production and distribution. Political instability undermines governance and investment, limiting the effectiveness of food assistance and development programs. Humanitarian crises, often compounded by environmental stress and economic decline, lead to prolonged food insecurity in affected regions.

Social and demographic changes also shape global food challenges. Migration, urbanization, and shifts in labor markets alter food demand and production capacity. At the same time, changing dietary preferences toward processed and animal-based foods increase environmental footprints. Ensuring sustainable consumption patterns alongside equitable access to nutritious food requires policy coherence, technological innovation, and inclusive governance to balance competing needs within the global food system.

Chapter 2: Agriculture, Sustainability, and Productivity

Agriculture is central to achieving sustainable development, as it underpins food security, livelihoods, and economic growth while directly influencing environmental health. The sector faces the complex challenge of increasing productivity to meet rising global food demand while minimizing ecological impacts and adapting to climate change. Balancing these objectives requires transforming agricultural systems to become more efficient, inclusive, and resilient.

Sustainable agriculture emphasizes the responsible management of natural resources, integration of ecosystem services, and adoption of technologies that enhance yields without degrading land and water systems. It recognizes that productivity gains must be pursued within ecological limits and supported by social equity. This transformation involves shifting from input-intensive models toward regenerative and circular approaches that restore soils, reduce emissions, and promote biodiversity.

This chapter examines the evolving role of agriculture in sustainable development, exploring pathways that align productivity growth with environmental sustainability and long-term food system resilience.

Transitioning to Sustainable Agricultural Systems

The transition to sustainable agricultural systems involves transforming how food is produced, managed, and distributed to ensure long-term productivity while conserving natural resources. It requires balancing economic viability with environmental stewardship and social equity. Conventional agricultural models, which prioritize short-term yield gains through intensive input use, have led to soil degradation, water scarcity, and biodiversity loss.

Sustainable systems seek to reverse these trends by promoting practices that maintain ecosystem health and resilience.

Central to this transition is the efficient use of natural resources. Sustainable agriculture emphasizes maintaining soil fertility through organic matter management, crop rotation, and reduced reliance on synthetic fertilizers. Water conservation practices such as precision irrigation and rainwater harvesting optimize resource use while reducing environmental impacts. The integration of livestock, crops, and forestry supports nutrient cycling and reduces waste within farming systems. These approaches create closed-loop systems that improve productivity and reduce dependency on external inputs.

Adopting diversified cropping systems is another key component of sustainability. Monocultures, while economically efficient in the short term, increase vulnerability to pests, diseases, and climate fluctuations. Crop diversification enhances resilience, stabilizes yields, and supports ecological balance. Incorporating legumes and cover crops improves soil structure and nitrogen levels, reducing the need for chemical fertilizers. Agroforestry systems, which combine trees and crops, contribute to carbon sequestration, erosion control, and microclimate regulation.

Technological innovation plays an important role in advancing sustainable agriculture. Precision farming tools, remote sensing, and data analytics enable farmers to optimize input use and monitor environmental conditions in real time. Mechanization and digital technologies improve labor efficiency and reduce waste. The application of biotechnology can enhance crop tolerance to drought, pests, and disease, supporting food production under changing climatic conditions. However, technology adoption must consider local capacities, access, and affordability to prevent widening inequalities among producers.

Policy frameworks and institutional support are critical for facilitating the shift toward sustainability. Governments can incentivize sustainable practices through subsidies, research investments, and land management programs that reward conservation outcomes. Certification schemes and market-based instruments such as eco-labeling promote accountability and consumer awareness. Strengthening agricultural extension services ensures knowledge transfer to farmers and supports adoption of best practices.

Social inclusion and community participation are essential to the success of sustainable agricultural transitions. Smallholder farmers, women, and youth often face barriers in accessing resources, credit, and technology. Empowering these groups enhances innovation and resilience at the local level. Collective action through cooperatives and farmer organizations improves access to markets and inputs, while participatory governance fosters accountability and transparency.

Transitioning to sustainable agricultural systems is not a uniform process but depends on local contexts, resource availability, and institutional capacities. It requires long-term commitment from governments, producers, and consumers to align agricultural policies, investments, and behaviors with principles that promote both productivity and ecological integrity.

Agroecology and Regenerative Practices

Agroecology and regenerative practices represent holistic approaches to agriculture that integrate ecological principles with farming systems to restore soil health, enhance biodiversity, and strengthen resilience. They promote sustainable production by aligning agricultural activities with natural processes rather than relying on external chemical inputs. These methods aim to create self-sustaining systems that maintain productivity while improving the environmental and social outcomes of food production.

Agroecology views agriculture as part of a larger ecosystem, emphasizing the interdependence of plants, animals, humans, and the environment. It combines traditional knowledge with modern science to develop context-specific solutions that work with, rather than against, nature. Key practices include polycultures, intercropping, and integrated pest management, which enhance soil fertility, control pests naturally, and increase ecosystem diversity. These techniques reduce reliance on synthetic fertilizers and pesticides, lowering production costs and minimizing environmental impacts.

Regenerative agriculture builds upon agroecological foundations by focusing on restoring degraded soils and enhancing carbon sequestration. It emphasizes practices that rebuild soil organic matter, improve water retention, and increase microbial activity. Techniques such as minimal tillage, composting, and rotational grazing contribute to the regeneration of soil structure and function. By maintaining living roots in the soil through cover cropping and diverse crop rotations, regenerative systems foster soil health and resilience to climatic variability.

Both agroecology and regenerative practices promote biodiversity as a key element of resilience. Diversified systems provide habitat for beneficial organisms such as pollinators and predators that support natural pest control. Increasing genetic diversity within crops reduces vulnerability to diseases and environmental stress. Maintaining on-farm biodiversity also contributes to the conservation of traditional crop varieties and livestock breeds, preserving cultural and ecological heritage.

Water management is another integral aspect of these practices. Agroecological systems enhance water efficiency by improving infiltration and reducing runoff through soil cover and organic matter accumulation. Regenerative approaches such as keyline design and contour farming help retain water in landscapes, reducing the need for irrigation. These strategies mitigate the risks of drought and flooding, supporting sustainable production under variable climatic conditions.

Social and economic dimensions are central to the success of agroecological and regenerative transitions. These practices prioritize local knowledge, community participation, and equitable resource access. They support smallholder farmers by promoting low-input systems that reduce financial risk and dependency on external suppliers. Localized food systems and shorter supply chains strengthen connections between producers and consumers, fostering transparency and shared responsibility in sustainable production.

Institutional support and policy integration determine the scale at which these practices can be implemented. Research, extension services, and incentive mechanisms are necessary to enable adoption and adaptation in diverse agricultural contexts. Collaboration between farmers, scientists, and policymakers helps align innovation with ecological and social goals. Agroecology and regenerative agriculture represent a shift toward systems thinking in food production, where ecological health and human well-being are mutually reinforcing outcomes of sustainable land management.

Soil Health and Resource Efficiency

Soil health underpins agricultural productivity, ecosystem stability, and food security. It refers to the capacity of soil to function as a living system that sustains plants, animals, and humans. Healthy soils regulate water, recycle nutrients, support biodiversity, and sequester carbon. Maintaining and improving soil health requires an understanding of its biological, chemical, and physical components, as well as how farming practices influence these interactions.

Intensive agricultural practices have degraded soil through erosion, compaction, salinization, and loss of organic matter. The overuse of synthetic fertilizers and pesticides has disrupted soil biology, reducing its ability to regenerate naturally. Sustainable soil management aims to reverse these effects by promoting practices that restore structure, enhance fertility, and maintain ecological balance. Conservation tillage, organic amendments, and crop diversification are key strategies that preserve soil integrity and prevent degradation.

Organic matter plays a critical role in maintaining soil function. It improves structure, increases water-holding capacity, and supports microbial activity essential for nutrient cycling. Adding compost, manure, and green manure contributes to long-term fertility while reducing the need for chemical inputs. Cover crops protect soil from erosion, fix nitrogen, and enhance carbon storage. By maintaining continuous vegetation cover, these practices also moderate soil temperature and moisture levels.

Nutrient management is central to resource efficiency in agriculture. Precision application of fertilizers and the use of nutrient budgeting tools help optimize input use while minimizing losses to the environment. Integrating organic and inorganic fertilizers balances immediate crop needs with long-term soil fertility. Rotations that include legumes naturally replenish nitrogen, reducing reliance on synthetic sources. Efficient nutrient use lowers production costs and mitigates environmental impacts such as eutrophication of water bodies.

Water management practices that enhance soil health and efficiency include contour farming, mulching, and maintaining vegetation cover. These techniques reduce runoff and improve infiltration, ensuring that rainfall and irrigation water are used effectively. Healthy soils with good structure and organic content store more water, buffering crops against drought. Efficient irrigation systems such as drip or sprinkler technologies further enhance water use efficiency and minimize waste.

Soil biodiversity supports essential ecological functions, including decomposition, nutrient cycling, and pest regulation. Encouraging biological diversity through reduced chemical use and habitat management enhances soil resilience to stress and disturbance. The presence of earthworms, fungi, and microorganisms contributes to nutrient mobilization and disease suppression, maintaining a balanced ecosystem within the soil.

Monitoring and assessment are important components of maintaining soil health and resource efficiency. Regular testing of soil properties helps farmers make informed decisions about input management and land use. Integrating traditional knowledge with modern soil science allows for adaptive management practices suited to local conditions. Strengthening soil health contributes to sustainable resource use, ensuring that agricultural landscapes remain productive and resilient under changing environmental conditions.

Climate-Smart Agriculture and Resilient Food Systems

Climate-smart agriculture (CSA) is an integrated approach that addresses the challenges of climate change while ensuring sustainable food production. It seeks to increase productivity, enhance resilience, and reduce greenhouse gas emissions across agricultural systems. The approach recognizes that climate change affects all dimensions of food security—availability, access, utilization, and stability—and requires adaptive practices that align with local environmental and socioeconomic contexts.

A key principle of CSA is improving resource efficiency to achieve higher yields with lower environmental impact. Practices such as precision agriculture, conservation tillage, and integrated nutrient management optimize input use and reduce waste. Crop diversification and intercropping strengthen resilience by spreading risk and maintaining productivity under variable climatic conditions. Efficient livestock management, including improved feed quality and manure treatment, reduces emissions while sustaining productivity.

Adaptation is central to CSA, ensuring that farming systems can withstand and recover from climate-related shocks. Adaptive practices include developing drought-tolerant and heat-resistant crop varieties, adjusting planting schedules, and diversifying income sources. Agroforestry and mixed farming systems create microclimates that buffer crops and livestock against temperature extremes. Restoring degraded lands and protecting watersheds enhance the natural resilience of ecosystems that support food production.

Mitigation within CSA focuses on reducing emissions and enhancing carbon sequestration. Increasing soil organic carbon through cover cropping, compost application, and reduced tillage contributes to climate regulation. Livestock and rice production systems are major sources of methane emissions, and targeted interventions such as improved feed efficiency and water management can significantly reduce their footprint. Integrating renewable energy technologies, such as solar-powered irrigation and biogas systems, also supports low-carbon agricultural development.

Resilient food systems extend beyond production to include post-harvest, processing, and distribution stages. Infrastructure that withstands extreme weather events, such as flood-resistant storage and transport networks, ensures continuity of food supply. Strengthening market access and value chains reduces the vulnerability of farmers to price volatility and income loss. Risk management tools, including crop insurance and early warning systems, help safeguard livelihoods during climate shocks.

Knowledge dissemination and capacity building are essential for implementing CSA effectively. Farmers need access to timely climate information, extension services, and training in adaptive practices. Collaboration between governments, research institutions, and local communities fosters innovation and the exchange of climate-resilient technologies. Digital platforms and mobile applications enhance information flow, allowing producers to make informed decisions under changing conditions.

Policy and institutional support provide the enabling environment for scaling CSA. Integrating climate objectives into agricultural policies, investment plans, and financial mechanisms aligns national strategies with global climate goals. Incentives for sustainable practices, climate finance, and public-private partnerships accelerate the transition to resilient food systems. Strengthening governance and coordination across sectors ensures that agriculture contributes to both adaptation and mitigation efforts in a balanced and equitable way.

Reducing Food Losses at the Production Level

Food losses at the production level occur during harvesting, handling, storage, and initial processing stages of the supply chain. These losses reduce the overall efficiency of food systems and undermine efforts to achieve food security and sustainability. Addressing them requires improving agricultural practices, infrastructure, and management systems to ensure that food produced reaches consumers without significant quantitative or qualitative degradation.

Harvesting practices play a critical role in minimizing losses. Poor timing, inadequate tools, and labor shortages can lead to damage or spoilage of crops. Training farmers in proper harvesting techniques, including optimal timing and handling, helps reduce mechanical damage and nutrient loss. Mechanization, when appropriately adapted to local conditions, can improve efficiency and consistency while reducing post-harvest waste. However, smallholder farmers often need access to credit and equipment-sharing schemes to adopt improved technologies.

Storage conditions are another major determinant of production-level food losses. Inadequate facilities expose produce to pests, mold, and moisture, leading to spoilage before it reaches the market. Introducing low-cost storage solutions such as hermetic bags, improved silos, and temperature-controlled environments can preserve food quality and extend shelf life. Proper drying and cleaning before storage also reduce contamination risks. Investment in rural infrastructure, particularly electricity and cold storage systems, enhances capacity to maintain perishable goods.

Post-harvest handling and transport are vulnerable stages where significant losses occur. Poor packaging, rough handling, and inefficient logistics contribute to bruising, contamination, and spillage. Developing standardized handling practices and using appropriate packaging materials help protect produce during transit. Road improvements and investment in transport networks shorten delivery times and reduce exposure to heat and humidity, particularly in tropical regions. Strengthening supply chain coordination among producers, traders, and transporters ensures that perishable items move quickly from farms to markets.

Quality standards and market structures influence the extent of food losses. When farmers cannot sell products due to strict appearance standards or market oversupply, edible food is often discarded. Establishing flexible grading systems that differentiate between cosmetic quality and nutritional value allows for the utilization of imperfect produce. Secondary markets, processing industries, and local food redistribution networks provide outlets for surplus and substandard crops that would otherwise go to waste.

Institutional and policy support are essential to scale loss-reduction efforts. Governments can promote awareness programs and provide training on best practices in harvesting and post-harvest management. Extension services that link farmers to innovation centers and technology providers enhance adoption of loss-prevention measures. Encouraging private sector investment in rural logistics and infrastructure strengthens the entire value chain. Data collection and monitoring systems help identify critical loss points and inform targeted interventions.

Reducing food losses at the production level not only improves food availability but also conserves resources such as land, water, and energy used in production. Efficient management of harvest and post-harvest stages contributes to more resilient and sustainable food systems capable of supporting growing populations under increasing environmental and economic pressures.

Chapter 3: Climate Change and Food System Resilience

Climate change presents one of the most significant threats to global food security, affecting every stage of the food system from production to consumption. Rising temperatures, shifting precipitation patterns, and the increasing frequency of extreme weather events are disrupting agricultural productivity, altering water availability, and threatening the livelihoods of millions of farmers. These changes intensify existing vulnerabilities, particularly in regions already facing food insecurity and environmental stress.

Building resilience within food systems is essential to manage climate risks and sustain productivity under changing conditions. Climate-resilient food systems emphasize diversification, adaptation, and sustainable resource management to reduce exposure to shocks and enhance recovery capacity. Integrating climate-smart agriculture, sustainable land use, and water-efficient technologies strengthens both environmental sustainability and food availability.

This chapter explores how climate change interacts with food systems, the adaptive measures necessary to safeguard food security, and the strategies that promote resilience in an increasingly unpredictable global climate.

Impacts of Climate Change on Food Production

Climate change is altering the conditions under which food is produced, with consequences for agricultural productivity, food availability, and global food security. Rising temperatures, changing precipitation patterns, and increased frequency of extreme weather events disrupt the delicate balance of ecosystems that support food production. These shifts affect crop yields, livestock health, fisheries, and the broader natural systems on which agriculture depends.

Temperature increases influence plant growth, crop development, and yield potential. In many regions, higher average temperatures accelerate crop maturation, shortening growing seasons and reducing productivity. Heat stress can impair pollination, decrease grain filling, and reduce nutrient content in staple crops such as wheat, rice, and maize. At the same time, warmer conditions may expand growing areas for some crops in higher latitudes, although gains are often offset by increased risks of pests, diseases, and water stress.

Changes in precipitation patterns affect the availability and reliability of water for agriculture. More frequent droughts limit irrigation potential and soil moisture, particularly in arid and semi-arid regions. Conversely, intense rainfall and flooding damage crops, erode soil, and destroy infrastructure. Irregular rainfall patterns make planting and harvesting schedules unpredictable, increasing uncertainty for farmers and affecting the stability of food supplies. In rain-fed agricultural systems, which sustain large portions of the global population, variability in rainfall directly translates into fluctuations in production.

Extreme weather events such as cyclones, heatwaves, and storms disrupt agricultural systems and infrastructure. These events destroy crops, livestock, and storage facilities, leading to immediate losses and long-term economic hardship. Recurrent natural disasters also discourage investment in agriculture, reducing productivity growth and resilience. The cumulative effects of repeated shocks weaken food systems and exacerbate vulnerability among smallholder farmers and rural communities.

Climate change also affects soil health and fertility. Increased temperatures and irregular rainfall contribute to soil erosion, nutrient depletion, and salinization in irrigated areas. Declining soil organic matter reduces water-holding capacity and nutrient cycling, making agricultural systems more susceptible to degradation. Desertification in dry regions and land degradation in humid zones further constrain productive capacity. Sustainable land management practices are essential to mitigate these impacts and preserve soil productivity.

Livestock systems are affected through reduced pasture quality, heat stress, and changes in disease distribution. Elevated temperatures reduce feed intake and fertility rates, leading to lower meat and milk yields. Shifts in vector-borne diseases and parasites affect animal health, increasing the need for veterinary interventions. Feed availability declines during droughts or prolonged dry seasons, creating competition between livestock and humans for limited resources.

Marine and freshwater fisheries face similar challenges as ocean warming and acidification alter aquatic ecosystems. Fish stocks migrate toward cooler waters, disrupting traditional fishing grounds and reducing catches for coastal communities. Coral bleaching and habitat loss threaten marine biodiversity and food supplies for millions of people dependent on fisheries.

The combined effects of these climate-related changes intensify the pressure on global food systems. Without adaptive measures, productivity declines, increased volatility, and shifting production zones will continue to challenge the capacity of agriculture to meet growing food demand.

Adaptation Strategies for Agricultural Resilience

Adaptation strategies for agricultural resilience aim to reduce the vulnerability of farming systems to climate variability and long-term environmental change. They involve modifying practices, technologies, and institutional frameworks to ensure that agricultural production remains stable under shifting climatic conditions. Effective adaptation enhances the capacity of farmers and food systems to anticipate, absorb, and recover from climatic shocks while maintaining productivity and sustainability.

Diversifying agricultural production is a key adaptation strategy that spreads risk across different crops, livestock, and income sources. Crop diversification reduces dependence on a single species and improves resilience to pests, diseases, and weather fluctuations.

Integrating livestock, aquaculture, and agroforestry systems enhances resource efficiency by linking production components through nutrient cycling and waste reuse. These diversified systems also stabilize income and provide alternative food sources during periods of stress.

Improved water management supports adaptation in regions facing increased drought or irregular rainfall. Techniques such as rainwater harvesting, drip irrigation, and deficit irrigation enhance water-use efficiency and help maintain yields during dry periods. On-farm water storage and soil moisture conservation practices, including mulching and contour farming, reduce runoff and increase infiltration. Developing water governance frameworks that promote equitable and sustainable allocation among sectors further strengthens resilience at the landscape scale.

Soil and land management practices are essential to building adaptive capacity. Conservation tillage, cover cropping, and organic matter incorporation improve soil structure and water retention while reducing erosion. Restoring degraded land through reforestation and controlled grazing restores ecological functions and enhances carbon sequestration. Maintaining healthy soils increases their ability to buffer against drought and flooding, sustaining agricultural productivity under variable climate conditions.

Climate-resilient crop varieties and livestock breeds form another critical component of adaptation. Breeding programs that focus on drought tolerance, heat resistance, and pest resilience provide options suited to evolving climatic conditions. Utilizing indigenous and traditional genetic resources supports adaptation by leveraging traits developed through long-term environmental exposure. Strengthening seed systems and ensuring farmers' access to high-quality planting materials facilitate widespread adoption of improved varieties.

Information systems and early warning mechanisms enable farmers to make informed decisions based on timely climate data. Seasonal forecasts, mobile-based advisories, and decision-support tools guide choices related to planting dates, irrigation scheduling, and pest management. Access to accurate information reduces uncertainty and allows proactive responses to climate risks. Extension services play a crucial role in communicating technical knowledge and facilitating farmer-to-farmer learning.

Financial mechanisms such as crop insurance, weather-indexed insurance, and credit facilities help buffer farmers against income loss from extreme events. These tools provide security that encourages investment in adaptive practices and technologies. Public and private sector partnerships can mobilize funding for resilience-building initiatives and infrastructure development.

Institutional and policy frameworks that integrate climate adaptation into agricultural planning support long-term transformation. Policies promoting land tenure security, capacity building, and research investment create enabling conditions for innovation. Coordination among sectors such as agriculture, water, and environment ensures coherence across adaptation measures, reducing trade-offs and strengthening systemic resilience.

Water, Energy, and Food Nexus Under Climate Stress

The water, energy, and food nexus represents the interdependence among three essential systems that sustain human life and economic development. Each sector relies on the others, with water required for food production and energy generation, energy needed for water treatment and agricultural processes, and food systems influencing both energy and water demand. Climate stress disrupts these linkages, amplifying competition for resources and exposing vulnerabilities in their management and governance.

Changes in precipitation and temperature directly affect water availability, influencing agricultural productivity and energy generation. Droughts reduce river flows and groundwater recharge, limiting irrigation capacity and hydroelectric output. Floods damage infrastructure and contaminate water sources, affecting both water quality and food safety. As variability in rainfall patterns increases, managing water allocation between agriculture, domestic use, and energy production becomes more complex, requiring adaptive and integrated approaches.

Energy systems are also sensitive to climatic variations. High temperatures increase cooling needs in power generation, while reduced water availability constrains thermal and hydroelectric plants that depend on water for cooling or power generation. In agriculture, energy is essential for pumping, processing, and transportation, making production vulnerable to energy price fluctuations and supply disruptions. Renewable energy technologies such as solar and wind offer opportunities to decouple agriculture from fossil fuel dependency and improve resilience, particularly in rural and off-grid regions.

Food production is one of the largest consumers of both water and energy resources. Agriculture accounts for most global freshwater withdrawals, and intensive production systems require significant energy inputs for fertilizers, machinery, and irrigation. Under climate stress, the efficiency of these inputs becomes critical to sustaining yields while minimizing emissions and water use. Adopting precision agriculture, low-energy irrigation systems, and circular approaches to resource reuse helps reduce intersectoral pressures.

Climate change intensifies competition among water, energy, and food sectors. Population growth and urbanization increase demand across all three systems, often in regions already facing scarcity. For example, expanding irrigation can improve food production but may reduce water availability for power generation or domestic supply. Similarly, large-scale bioenergy projects compete with food crops for land and water resources. Balancing these competing demands requires coordinated policy frameworks that integrate environmental, social, and economic objectives.

Governance plays a pivotal role in managing the nexus under climate stress. Fragmented institutional responsibilities often lead to conflicting policies and inefficient resource allocation. Integrated resource management approaches encourage cross-sectoral planning and promote synergies between water, energy, and food systems. Data sharing, stakeholder participation, and transparent decision-making processes enhance coordination and accountability.

Technological innovation supports more efficient and resilient nexus management. Wastewater reuse, desalination powered by renewable energy, and nutrient recovery from agricultural residues illustrate how systems integration can reduce environmental impacts. Investment in infrastructure and capacity building strengthens adaptive capacity, while policy coherence across sectors ensures that climate adaptation strategies contribute to long-term sustainability and equitable access to essential resources.

Managing Extreme Events and Food Supply Chains

Extreme weather events such as droughts, floods, hurricanes, and heatwaves increasingly disrupt food systems, threatening production, processing, and distribution. These events can destroy crops, damage infrastructure, and disrupt market access, creating volatility in food availability and prices. Managing their impact requires strengthening the resilience of supply chains through improved planning, infrastructure, and governance.

Preparedness is the foundation of effective management. Early warning systems that combine meteorological forecasting, satellite monitoring, and local data enable governments and producers to anticipate risks and implement preventive measures. Integrating risk information into agricultural planning allows farmers to adjust planting schedules, select resilient crop varieties, and diversify production systems. Investment in local weather stations and data-sharing networks enhances decision-making and coordination among stakeholders.

Infrastructure resilience is essential to sustaining food supply during extreme events. Roads, storage facilities, and transport networks are often the most affected components of the food system. Designing infrastructure that can withstand floods and high temperatures reduces disruptions and losses. Building elevated storage units, reinforcing supply corridors, and improving drainage systems help maintain continuity in food transport and distribution. Public investment in rural infrastructure complements private sector logistics to strengthen supply chain connectivity.

Diversification of supply sources and markets mitigates disruptions when extreme events affect specific regions. Encouraging decentralized food processing and local procurement reduces dependency on distant suppliers and enhances adaptability. Regional cooperation can improve trade flexibility, allowing surplus areas to support those facing shortages. Policy frameworks that facilitate emergency trade flows and reduce export restrictions during crises help stabilize markets and prevent scarcity.

Financial risk management tools provide support for producers and businesses affected by climate-related shocks. Crop insurance, weather-indexed insurance, and contingency funds protect livelihoods and reduce the need for ad hoc disaster assistance. Financial institutions play a role in promoting recovery through accessible credit for rehabilitation of damaged infrastructure and replanting. Risk-sharing mechanisms that involve public, private, and community actors strengthen economic resilience across the supply chain.

Supply chain transparency and traceability enhance the ability to respond quickly during disruptions. Digital technologies, including blockchain and remote sensing, enable real-time monitoring of production and logistics. These systems support targeted interventions, such as rerouting supplies or activating emergency reserves. Coordinated communication among producers, processors, distributors, and authorities ensures that resources are deployed efficiently and equitably during crises.

Humanitarian and food assistance systems form a critical safety net in managing extreme events. Strategic grain reserves, emergency food stocks, and community-based distribution systems ensure timely access to essential food supplies. Strengthening institutional coordination between agricultural, disaster management, and social protection agencies enables a faster and more coherent response. Integrating risk management into food system planning ensures that short-term recovery measures contribute to long-term resilience and stability.

Integrating Climate Risk into Food Policy

Integrating climate risk into food policy involves aligning agricultural, environmental, and economic strategies with an understanding of the long-term impacts of climate change. It ensures that food systems are managed in ways that anticipate and reduce vulnerability to climatic shocks while maintaining productivity and equity. Policies that incorporate climate risk assessment provide a foundation for sustainable development by linking adaptation, mitigation, and resilience objectives within the broader context of food security.

A key step in this integration is the development of risk-informed decision-making frameworks. Governments and institutions require reliable climate data and scenario modeling to assess potential impacts on crops, livestock, water availability, and markets. These assessments help identify vulnerable regions and populations, enabling targeted interventions. Incorporating climate projections into agricultural planning and national food strategies ensures that resource allocation and policy priorities reflect future environmental conditions rather than historical trends.

Adaptation policies form a central element of climate risk integration. Agricultural policies should support the adoption of climate-resilient practices, including drought-tolerant crops, diversified farming systems, and improved water management. Incentive mechanisms such as subsidies for conservation practices or low-interest loans for adaptive technologies encourage innovation and reduce the costs of transition for farmers. Integrating adaptation into national development plans strengthens coherence across sectors, ensuring that agriculture, water, and energy policies reinforce each other under changing climatic conditions.

Mitigation policies contribute to managing climate risks by reducing the emissions that drive environmental degradation. Integrating mitigation objectives into food policy requires promoting sustainable production methods, such as low-emission livestock systems and reduced reliance on chemical fertilizers. Encouraging circular economy models, renewable energy use, and sustainable supply chains helps lower the carbon footprint of food systems. Aligning agricultural policies with national climate commitments supports compliance with international frameworks, including the Paris Agreement.

Institutional coordination enhances the effectiveness of climate-informed food policies. Ministries responsible for agriculture, environment, finance, and social welfare must collaborate to ensure policy coherence and avoid trade-offs between growth and sustainability. Establishing inter-ministerial committees, technical working groups, and data-sharing mechanisms strengthens cross-sectoral alignment. Decentralized governance structures can also support localized risk management, where regional and community-level authorities adapt policies to specific environmental and socioeconomic conditions.

Investment in research, education, and capacity building underpins the successful integration of climate risk into policy. Expanding agricultural research on resilient crops, sustainable resource management, and ecosystem-based adaptation provides evidence for informed policy decisions. Training programs for farmers and policymakers enhance understanding of climate risks and practical adaptation options. Public awareness campaigns promote behavioral change, linking consumer choices and sustainable production practices to broader climate objectives.

Financial and market instruments support the operationalization of climate-resilient food policies. Climate finance, green bonds, and risk-sharing mechanisms mobilize resources for adaptation and mitigation initiatives. Integrating climate risk criteria into agricultural investment frameworks ensures that financial flows support resilience-building efforts rather than increasing exposure to environmental hazards. Monitoring and evaluation systems that track climate-related outcomes allow policymakers to refine strategies and maintain alignment with evolving climatic realities.

Chapter 4: Nutrition, Health, and Sustainable Diets

Nutrition and health are essential components of food security and sustainable development. Access to sufficient food alone does not guarantee well-being; the quality, diversity, and nutritional value of diets determine long-term health outcomes. Malnutrition in all its forms—undernutrition, micronutrient deficiencies, overweight, and obesity—poses significant challenges to societies and health systems. Addressing these challenges requires a comprehensive understanding of the links between food systems, nutrition, and public health.

Sustainable diets promote human health while minimizing environmental impacts, ensuring that food production and consumption patterns remain within planetary boundaries. They integrate nutritional adequacy with ecological balance, emphasizing whole foods, reduced waste, and responsible resource use. Culturally sensitive and locally adapted dietary approaches strengthen community resilience and social acceptance.

This chapter examines how nutrition and health intersect with sustainable food systems, highlighting the transition toward sustainable diets that support both population well-being and environmental sustainability.

From Hunger to Malnutrition: The Double Burden

The global food landscape has shifted from one dominated by hunger and undernutrition to a more complex scenario where malnutrition takes multiple forms. The double burden of malnutrition refers to the coexistence of undernutrition and overnutrition within individuals, households, and populations. This phenomenon highlights the changing dynamics of food systems and the need for policies that address both nutrient deficiencies and diet-related chronic diseases simultaneously.

Undernutrition persists in many low- and middle-income countries, particularly where poverty, conflict, and environmental degradation limit access to sufficient and diverse food. It manifests as stunting, wasting, and micronutrient deficiencies, particularly among children and women. Insufficient dietary intake, poor health conditions, and inadequate sanitation contribute to these outcomes. Undernourished populations are more vulnerable to disease and experience reduced cognitive and physical development, which limits economic productivity and perpetuates poverty cycles.

At the same time, overnutrition and obesity are rising rapidly, even in regions still struggling with hunger. Increased urbanization, income growth, and shifts in dietary habits have led to greater consumption of processed foods high in fats, sugars, and salt. Sedentary lifestyles further contribute to weight gain and metabolic disorders such as diabetes, hypertension, and cardiovascular disease. These trends place significant burdens on healthcare systems and reduce quality of life across diverse socioeconomic groups.

The coexistence of these forms of malnutrition often occurs within the same community or household. A child may suffer from stunting due to nutrient deficiencies, while an adult in the same family may experience obesity linked to poor dietary quality. Food environments that promote inexpensive but calorie-dense products exacerbate this imbalance. Limited access to fresh fruits, vegetables, and protein sources forces many households to rely on affordable but nutritionally poor options.

Economic and social transitions influence the double burden of malnutrition. As economies grow, traditional diets based on grains and legumes are increasingly replaced by diets rich in animal products, refined carbohydrates, and processed foods. Global trade and marketing accelerate these dietary shifts, shaping preferences and availability. Food systems designed to maximize volume and efficiency often fail to prioritize nutritional value, creating disparities between food quantity and quality.

Policy responses must address structural factors driving both hunger and overnutrition. Strengthening social protection programs ensures vulnerable populations have access to nutritious foods. Integrating nutrition education into health and agricultural policies promotes awareness of balanced diets. Reforming food subsidies to favor fresh produce and whole grains can shift consumption patterns toward healthier options.

Investments in public health, urban planning, and sustainable food production contribute to reducing the double burden. Ensuring equitable access to safe water, sanitation, and healthcare complements efforts to improve nutrition. Coordinated action among governments, private sectors, and civil society supports the development of food environments that promote both health and sustainability.

Nutrition-Sensitive Agriculture and Policy Integration

Nutrition-sensitive agriculture seeks to enhance the contribution of food systems to improved nutrition outcomes by addressing both the quantity and quality of food produced and consumed. It focuses on making agricultural policies, programs, and investments more responsive to nutritional needs. This approach recognizes that food production alone does not guarantee healthy diets and that aligning agriculture with nutrition objectives requires cross-sectoral coordination and policy coherence.

Integrating nutrition into agricultural planning begins with promoting the production and availability of diverse and nutrient-rich foods. Encouraging crop diversification, including fruits, vegetables, legumes, and biofortified staples, enhances the nutritional value of local diets. Livestock, aquaculture, and horticulture programs can complement traditional cereal production by providing essential sources of protein and micronutrients. Supporting smallholder farmers to cultivate nutrient-dense crops improves both household food security and community dietary diversity.

Access to nutritious food depends not only on production but also on income and market structures. Nutrition-sensitive agricultural programs emphasize improving rural livelihoods, particularly for women, who play a central role in food production and household nutrition. Providing women with access to land, inputs, and extension services increases productivity and strengthens their decision-making power in food and health-related matters. Linking farmers to markets through cooperatives and value-chain development ensures that nutritious foods reach consumers efficiently.

Policy integration is essential to sustain nutrition-sensitive agriculture. Agricultural, health, education, and social protection policies must align around shared objectives that promote food and nutrition security. Coordinated policy frameworks encourage the inclusion of nutrition goals in agricultural strategies, ensuring that interventions target both economic and health outcomes. For example, aligning school feeding programs with local agricultural production can stimulate markets for smallholders while improving children's dietary intake.

Public investments in research and innovation play a key role in linking agriculture and nutrition. Breeding programs for nutrient-rich and climate-resilient crops, such as iron-rich beans or vitamin A-enriched sweet potatoes, help address micronutrient deficiencies. Extension services and farmer training programs disseminate knowledge on nutrition-sensitive practices, including sustainable soil management, safe food handling, and dietary diversification. Partnerships between research institutions, governments, and the private sector accelerate the scaling up of these innovations.

Information and awareness are critical components of nutrition-sensitive approaches. Nutrition education integrated into agricultural programs helps households understand the importance of balanced diets and food preparation methods that retain nutrient value. Public communication campaigns promoting healthy eating behaviors can complement supply-side interventions by stimulating demand for nutritious foods.

Monitoring and evaluation systems are necessary to measure the nutritional impacts of agricultural policies and programs. Indicators that track dietary diversity, micronutrient intake, and household food security enable policymakers to assess progress and refine strategies. Integrating these metrics into agricultural monitoring frameworks ensures accountability and continuous improvement.

Financing mechanisms that prioritize nutrition outcomes within agricultural investments reinforce long-term sustainability. Incentives for private sector engagement in producing and marketing healthy foods expand access and affordability. Inclusive policy integration ensures that agriculture contributes not only to economic growth but also to the well-being and nutritional health of populations.

Sustainable Diets and Cultural Dimensions of Food

Sustainable diets aim to promote human health while minimizing environmental impacts and preserving cultural traditions. They are defined by their ability to meet nutritional needs, support ecosystems, and ensure economic and social equity. The transition toward sustainable diets requires balancing global sustainability goals with the diverse cultural and regional contexts that shape food preferences, production systems, and consumption patterns.

Cultural values and traditions influence how food is produced, prepared, and consumed. These practices reflect local ecological conditions, historical development, and community identity. In many societies, traditional diets emphasize seasonal and locally sourced foods that align with environmental sustainability. However, modernization, globalization, and urbanization have altered these patterns, leading to increased consumption of processed and resource-intensive foods. Maintaining cultural diversity in diets supports both social continuity and ecological resilience.

Environmental considerations are central to sustainable diets. Food production contributes significantly to greenhouse gas emissions, land degradation, and water use. Diets high in animal-based products generally have greater environmental footprints than plant-based diets. Shifting toward diets that emphasize plant-based foods, whole grains, and legumes can reduce environmental pressures. At the same time, sustainability strategies must respect regional contexts, as livestock and fisheries remain vital to the livelihoods and nutrition of many communities.

Health outcomes are closely tied to dietary sustainability. Diets dominated by processed foods and refined sugars increase the prevalence of obesity, diabetes, and cardiovascular diseases. Promoting balanced diets rich in fruits, vegetables, and minimally processed foods improves public health while supporting sustainable production systems. Integrating nutrition education into agricultural and public health programs encourages consumers to make informed choices aligned with sustainability goals.

Economic accessibility determines the feasibility of adopting sustainable diets. Nutrient-rich and environmentally friendly foods are often more expensive or less available in low-income regions. Policies that improve market access, reduce food loss, and support small-scale producers can lower costs and increase the availability of sustainable options. Strengthening local food systems enhances resilience to global market fluctuations and ensures that sustainability efforts benefit producers and consumers alike.

Social equity and inclusion are integral to the cultural dimensions of sustainable diets. Food systems must ensure fair wages, safe working conditions, and equitable access to resources. Empowering women and marginalized groups enhances decision-making and innovation in food production and consumption. Recognizing the social significance of food fosters community engagement in sustainability transitions.

Public policy and education play essential roles in aligning cultural and environmental objectives. Food-based dietary guidelines that integrate sustainability considerations provide a framework for promoting healthier and more sustainable eating habits. Collaboration among governments, civil society, and the private sector supports food systems that respect cultural diversity while advancing environmental and nutritional goals.

Food Safety and Public Health

Food safety and public health are closely linked components of sustainable food systems. Safe food prevents illness, supports nutritional well-being, and contributes to economic stability. Foodborne diseases caused by bacteria, viruses, parasites, and chemical contaminants pose serious risks to human health and undermine confidence in food supply chains. Effective food safety management requires coordinated action across production, processing, transport, and consumption stages to minimize risks and ensure compliance with standards.

Contamination can occur at any point in the food chain. Poor agricultural practices, unsafe handling, and inadequate processing or storage create conditions that allow pathogens to spread. The use of contaminated water for irrigation, overuse of pesticides, and poor hygiene during harvesting and transport further increase risk. Strengthening biosecurity measures and implementing good agricultural and manufacturing practices reduce contamination and improve overall food safety.

Public health systems play a critical role in monitoring and responding to foodborne illnesses. Surveillance programs track outbreaks and identify sources of contamination, enabling timely interventions. Laboratory testing and data-sharing networks between health and food authorities enhance the capacity to detect hazards. Transparent reporting and public communication support consumer trust and encourage preventive measures among producers and retailers.

Regulatory frameworks provide the foundation for food safety governance. Standards established by organizations such as the

Codex Alimentarius Commission guide national regulations on contaminants, additives, and labeling. Effective enforcement depends on coordination among ministries of health, agriculture, and trade, as well as adequate inspection capacity. Risk-based approaches prioritize control measures where hazards are most likely to occur, improving efficiency and resource allocation.

Globalization of food trade introduces new challenges for food safety. The movement of food across borders increases exposure to diverse production systems and regulatory standards. Harmonizing international regulations, improving traceability, and strengthening border inspection systems reduce risks associated with imported and exported goods. Collaboration among countries through information exchange and joint monitoring enhances food safety in interconnected markets.

Consumer awareness and education are essential components of public health protection. Knowledge of safe food handling, cooking temperatures, and storage practices helps prevent illness at the household level. Public information campaigns and nutrition programs reinforce healthy behaviors and highlight the importance of hygiene. Encouraging demand for certified and quality-assured products incentivizes producers to maintain high safety standards.

Technological innovation supports advances in food safety management. Rapid diagnostic testing, digital tracking systems, and data analytics improve detection and response times. Blockchain technology enhances traceability by recording every step in the supply chain, increasing transparency and accountability. Investment in infrastructure such as cold storage and sanitation facilities ensures that perishable foods remain safe throughout transport and distribution.

Climate change and urbanization introduce additional pressures on food safety. Rising temperatures can increase pathogen proliferation, while extreme weather events disrupt supply chains and storage conditions. Urban growth strains sanitation systems, increasing contamination risks in informal markets. Integrating food safety considerations into climate adaptation and urban planning strengthens resilience and safeguards public health outcomes.

Promoting Equity and Access to Nutritious Food

Equity and access to nutritious food are essential components of sustainable food systems. Ensuring that all individuals can obtain sufficient, safe, and nutritious food requires addressing structural inequalities that affect availability, affordability, and utilization. Disparities in income, geography, gender, and social status shape people's ability to secure healthy diets. Food policies that promote inclusivity and justice strengthen the foundations of long-term food security and social stability.

Economic inequality remains one of the most significant barriers to food access. Low-income households often spend a large proportion of their income on food, making them vulnerable to price fluctuations and market disruptions. Limited access to credit, land, and productive resources further constrains their capacity to produce or purchase adequate food. Targeted social protection measures, such as cash transfers, food subsidies, and nutrition assistance programs, can reduce economic barriers and enhance purchasing power for vulnerable populations.

Geographical disparities influence both food production and access. Rural communities may experience isolation from major markets, while urban areas face challenges in ensuring affordability and availability of fresh foods. Investments in transportation infrastructure, storage facilities, and local markets help bridge these gaps. Strengthening rural-urban linkages supports more efficient food distribution and enables producers to access broader consumer networks. Decentralized food systems that rely on local supply chains reduce dependency on distant markets and increase resilience to external shocks.

Gender inequality also limits access to nutritious food. Women play a central role in food production, processing, and preparation, yet often face discrimination in land ownership, credit access, and decision-making. Empowering women through education, capacity building, and policy reforms enhances household nutrition outcomes. Ensuring that women have equal opportunities to participate in agricultural value chains improves both productivity and equity in food systems.

Cultural and social factors influence dietary practices and access to diverse foods. Marginalized groups, including ethnic minorities and indigenous populations, may have distinct food traditions that are not supported by mainstream markets or agricultural policies. Recognizing and integrating traditional food systems into national food strategies preserves cultural diversity and promotes inclusive development. Policies that respect cultural preferences and local food heritage foster participation and ownership in food system transformation.

Public health policies contribute to equitable access by ensuring that nutritious foods are both available and affordable. Regulation of food pricing, fortification programs, and support for small-scale producers help balance market forces and improve the nutritional quality of food supplies. Nutrition education and awareness campaigns empower consumers to make healthier choices while addressing misinformation about diet and food safety.

Governance frameworks must promote collaboration across sectors to achieve equity in food access. Integrating food, health, and social policies allows governments to address multiple dimensions of inequality simultaneously. Transparent and participatory decision-making processes ensure that the voices of marginalized communities are represented. Strengthening institutional accountability and investing in data collection on food access and nutrition outcomes support evidence-based policymaking that prioritizes fairness and inclusion.

Chapter 5: Governance, Institutions, and Policy Frameworks

Governance and institutional frameworks form the backbone of sustainable food security, shaping how decisions are made, resources are managed, and policies are implemented. As food systems become increasingly interconnected, effective governance ensures coordination across sectors such as agriculture, environment, trade, and health. Institutions play a critical role in translating global commitments into national and local action, facilitating collaboration among governments, the private sector, and civil society.

Sound policy frameworks provide the direction needed to balance economic growth, environmental sustainability, and social inclusion. They establish the regulatory and institutional conditions under which sustainable food systems can thrive, promoting transparency, accountability, and equitable participation. Integrating food security into broader development agendas enhances policy coherence and effectiveness.

This chapter explores the roles of governance, institutions, and policy frameworks in achieving sustainable food security, emphasizing coordination, inclusivity, and adaptive policymaking across multiple levels of governance.

Global Governance of Food Security

Global governance of food security involves the collective efforts of international organizations, governments, civil society, and the private sector to coordinate actions that ensure stable and equitable access to food worldwide. It provides the frameworks, policies, and institutions necessary to address complex challenges such as hunger, trade inequities, climate change, and resource scarcity. Effective governance aligns global commitments with national implementation, fostering cooperation among diverse actors.

The foundation of global food governance rests on multilateral institutions that establish norms and coordinate policy responses. The Food and Agriculture Organization of the United Nations leads efforts to eradicate hunger and promote sustainable agricultural practices. The World Food Programme addresses emergency food assistance and resilience-building in vulnerable regions. The International Fund for Agricultural Development supports rural development and smallholder farmers through financial and technical assistance. Together, these organizations guide the global agenda on food security and sustainable agriculture.

The Committee on World Food Security serves as a central platform for inclusive policy dialogue. It brings together governments, civil society, private sector representatives, and research institutions to develop guidelines and principles that promote food security and nutrition. Its policy frameworks, such as the Voluntary Guidelines on the Right to Food and the Principles for Responsible Investment in Agriculture and Food Systems, provide reference points for national and international actions. The committee's inclusive approach ensures that diverse perspectives shape global governance outcomes.

Trade governance significantly influences global food security. The World Trade Organization establishes rules that govern the movement of agricultural goods, influencing market stability, food prices, and access for importing nations. Balancing trade liberalization with food sovereignty remains a persistent challenge, particularly for developing countries that depend on imports or face competition from subsidized agricultural exports. Regional trade agreements increasingly include provisions related to food security, sustainable development, and climate adaptation.

Financial and development institutions also play a role in global food governance. The World Bank, regional development banks, and international funds mobilize resources for agricultural investment, infrastructure, and innovation. Initiatives such as the Global Agriculture and Food Security Program support smallholder farmers and enhance resilience to shocks. Aligning financial flows with sustainability objectives ensures that global investment contributes to long-term food system transformation.

Climate change and environmental degradation have shifted governance priorities toward resilience and sustainability. International frameworks such as the Paris Agreement and the 2030 Agenda for Sustainable Development emphasize the interconnection between food security, climate action, and biodiversity conservation. Global cooperation on climate-resilient agriculture and low-carbon food systems is increasingly integrated into national commitments and development programs.

Civil society and non-governmental organizations contribute to governance by advocating for equity, transparency, and accountability. They influence global policy through research, monitoring, and capacity building at the community level. Private sector participation is also expanding, particularly in sustainable supply chains and innovation partnerships. Effective global governance depends on maintaining a balance between public oversight and private engagement to ensure that actions serve collective interests and uphold the right to adequate food.

National Policy Frameworks and Institutional Coordination

National policy frameworks for food security provide the foundation for achieving sustainable, equitable, and resilient food systems. These frameworks define government priorities, establish institutional responsibilities, and guide investments across agriculture, health, environment, and social protection sectors. Effective coordination among ministries and agencies ensures coherence between policies and avoids duplication or conflict among initiatives.

Developing comprehensive food security strategies requires integrating goals related to availability, access, utilization, and stability. Many countries adopt national food and nutrition security policies that align with global commitments such as the Sustainable Development Goals. These policies often include measures to improve agricultural productivity, enhance rural livelihoods, and strengthen nutrition outcomes. Coordination mechanisms facilitate the alignment of sectoral programs and ensure that food security objectives are embedded in broader economic and development planning.

Institutional arrangements play a central role in implementing food security policies. Inter-ministerial committees or councils are commonly established to oversee coordination among agriculture, health, trade, and environment ministries. These bodies support decision-making, monitoring, and resource allocation while ensuring that national policies address both short-term needs and long-term sustainability. Clear mandates and accountability mechanisms are essential to maintain institutional effectiveness and policy continuity.

Decentralization strengthens implementation by bringing decision-making closer to local communities. Local governments often have greater understanding of regional needs, resource constraints, and production conditions. Empowering subnational authorities with technical and financial resources enhances responsiveness and adaptability. Coordination between national and local levels ensures that policy frameworks remain flexible and inclusive while maintaining alignment with national priorities.

Cross-sectoral policy integration is necessary to manage the interconnections between agriculture, water, energy, and environment. Policies promoting irrigation expansion, for example, must consider water availability and ecosystem impacts. Similarly, nutrition objectives should be integrated into agricultural planning and rural development programs. Regular inter-agency consultations, joint planning exercises, and shared data systems support harmonization across sectors.

Public participation and stakeholder engagement improve the legitimacy and effectiveness of policy frameworks. Involving farmers, civil society organizations, research institutions, and the private sector allows for diverse perspectives and innovation. Multi-stakeholder platforms facilitate collaboration, knowledge exchange, and joint problem-solving. Inclusivity ensures that policies reflect the needs of different groups, particularly smallholders, women, and marginalized populations.

Monitoring and evaluation systems are vital for tracking progress and identifying gaps in implementation. Indicators that measure agricultural output, food access, and nutrition outcomes provide evidence for policy adjustments. Regular reporting promotes transparency and accountability, enabling governments to refine strategies based on changing conditions. Data integration across institutions enhances the capacity to respond to emerging challenges such as climate impacts or market disruptions.

Sustainable financing underpins national food security frameworks. Aligning budget allocations with strategic priorities ensures consistent funding for key programs such as agricultural extension, infrastructure development, and social protection. Partnerships with international organizations and development banks mobilize additional resources and technical expertise. Effective coordination among institutions and stakeholders ensures that policies remain coherent, evidence-based, and adaptable to evolving food system dynamics.

Role of Local Governments and Community-Based Systems

Local governments and community-based systems play a critical role in achieving food security by implementing policies and programs that address local needs and conditions. Their proximity to communities allows them to identify vulnerabilities, manage resources effectively, and support inclusive participation in decision-making. Decentralized governance enables context-specific approaches to food production, distribution, and consumption that complement national strategies.

Local governments often serve as the primary link between national policy frameworks and communities. They are responsible for implementing agricultural development programs, managing rural infrastructure, and supporting small-scale farmers. Through local planning processes, they can integrate food security considerations into broader development agendas, including land use, water management, and health initiatives. Strengthening institutional capacity at the local level ensures effective coordination and resource allocation.

Community-based systems contribute to food security through grassroots engagement, collective action, and local knowledge. Farmer cooperatives, water user associations, and women's groups facilitate access to resources, information, and markets. These organizations promote sustainable agricultural practices, improve bargaining power, and enhance resilience to environmental and economic shocks. Community-led initiatives in seed saving, agroecology, and natural resource management help maintain biodiversity and sustain local food systems.

Social protection and nutrition programs benefit from the involvement of local governments and community organizations. They play a vital role in identifying vulnerable households, distributing food assistance, and implementing school feeding or public works schemes. Local authorities are well positioned to monitor conditions on the ground and adapt interventions to seasonal or climatic changes. Partnerships between local administrations and civil society improve targeting efficiency and reduce administrative delays.

Local food systems are strengthened when municipalities support short supply chains and urban-rural linkages. Urban agriculture initiatives, farmers' markets, and local procurement policies enhance access to fresh and nutritious food in cities while providing income opportunities for rural producers. Integrating food security goals into urban planning contributes to sustainable city development and reduces dependency on long-distance supply chains.

Capacity building is essential to enhance the effectiveness of local governments in addressing food security. Training programs on planning, budgeting, and monitoring equip local officials with the skills needed to implement complex, cross-sectoral initiatives. Strengthening data collection and management at the local level supports evidence-based decision-making. Partnerships with universities and research institutions can provide technical expertise and innovative solutions adapted to local realities.

Inclusive governance is a defining feature of successful community-based food systems. Participatory planning processes allow communities to voice priorities, influence policy decisions, and monitor outcomes. Transparency and accountability mechanisms foster trust and ensure equitable distribution of benefits. Empowering marginalized groups, including women, youth, and indigenous populations, enhances social cohesion and strengthens local resilience.

Collaboration between local and national institutions ensures coherence across scales. Local governments act as intermediaries in coordinating projects funded by national agencies or international donors. Effective communication and resource-sharing mechanisms between levels of government prevent duplication and enhance impact. Integrating community-based initiatives into formal governance structures creates stronger, more adaptive systems capable of addressing food security challenges in diverse environments.

International Cooperation and Multilateral Mechanisms

International cooperation and multilateral mechanisms are essential for addressing the global dimensions of food security. The interconnected nature of food systems means that challenges such as climate change, trade disruptions, and resource scarcity transcend national borders. Collaborative governance ensures that countries can coordinate responses, share knowledge, and mobilize resources to strengthen resilience and achieve equitable access to food.

Multilateral institutions provide the platforms through which countries align their policies and actions. The United Nations system, particularly the Food and Agriculture Organization, the World Food Programme, and the International Fund for Agricultural Development, facilitates cooperation on agricultural development, nutrition, and humanitarian assistance. These organizations support capacity building, technical assistance, and the implementation of global frameworks such as the Sustainable Development Goals. Their coordination helps harmonize efforts and avoid duplication among development partners.

International agreements establish the normative foundations for cooperation. The Universal Declaration on the Eradication of Hunger and Malnutrition, the World Food Summit commitments, and the Paris Agreement on climate change outline shared goals and principles that guide national actions. These frameworks promote accountability and transparency by setting measurable targets and encouraging periodic reporting. Global conventions on biodiversity, desertification, and water resources also influence food security policies by promoting sustainable resource management.

Trade plays a central role in global food security, and multilateral mechanisms under the World Trade Organization shape the rules governing agricultural markets. Trade liberalization can enhance food availability by improving market access, but it can also expose producers and consumers to volatility. International cooperation is necessary to ensure that trade policies do not undermine food sovereignty or disadvantage smallholder farmers. Initiatives such as regional trade agreements and South-South cooperation enhance market integration while supporting local production and resilience.

Humanitarian cooperation forms a key aspect of the global food security architecture. The World Food Programme and international nongovernmental organizations provide emergency food assistance in response to conflicts, natural disasters, and economic crises. Coordination among humanitarian actors ensures efficient resource distribution and minimizes overlaps. Global partnerships, including the Global Network Against Food Crises, promote early warning systems and joint planning to prevent and address acute food insecurity.

Financial cooperation through multilateral development banks and global funds mobilizes investment in agriculture, infrastructure, and innovation. Mechanisms such as the Global Agriculture and Food Security Program and the Green Climate Fund channel resources toward projects that enhance productivity, reduce emissions, and strengthen adaptation to climate impacts. International financing complements domestic budgets and private investment, supporting long-term transformation of food systems.

Research and knowledge exchange are facilitated through international cooperation networks that link governments, academia, and civil society. Collaborative research initiatives focus on improving crop resilience, reducing post-harvest losses, and developing sustainable farming technologies. Platforms such as the Global Forum on Agricultural Research and Innovation promote information sharing and foster inclusive participation from developing countries.

Diplomatic engagement and global summits reinforce political commitment to food security. Regular meetings of international bodies, including the Committee on World Food Security, provide opportunities for dialogue, negotiation, and review of progress. Through coordinated multilateral action, countries align priorities and build partnerships that support a more stable and equitable global food system.

Accountability, Monitoring, and Policy Coherence

Accountability, monitoring, and policy coherence are fundamental to ensuring that food security initiatives achieve their intended outcomes and remain aligned with broader development objectives. Transparent systems of governance, clear performance indicators, and coordinated policy frameworks enable governments and stakeholders to track progress, evaluate impact, and adjust strategies based on evidence.

Accountability mechanisms establish the standards and processes through which institutions are held responsible for implementing food security policies and programs. These mechanisms promote transparency in decision-making and resource allocation. Parliamentary oversight, independent audits, and public reporting increase confidence in government actions. Multi-stakeholder platforms that include civil society, academia, and the private sector further strengthen accountability by providing avenues for participation and feedback.

Monitoring systems are essential tools for assessing performance and identifying areas for improvement. They collect and analyze data on food availability, access, utilization, and stability. Reliable monitoring frameworks depend on well-defined indicators that reflect both short-term and long-term dimensions of food security. Integrating data from agricultural, health, and social sectors allows policymakers to capture the interconnections between nutrition, production, and economic development. Advances in digital technology, such as remote sensing and geospatial analysis, enhance the accuracy and timeliness of monitoring processes.

Evaluation complements monitoring by assessing the effectiveness, efficiency, and sustainability of interventions. Periodic evaluations provide evidence on what works and what does not, enabling adaptive management. Independent evaluations conducted by external experts or international organizations add credibility to findings and support policy learning. Sharing evaluation results across institutions fosters knowledge exchange and contributes to global efforts to improve food governance.

Policy coherence ensures that different sectors and levels of government work toward consistent objectives without creating contradictions or inefficiencies. Food security policies intersect with agriculture, trade, environment, health, and social protection, requiring coordination across ministries and agencies. Coherent policy frameworks prevent negative spillovers, such as agricultural subsidies that harm nutrition outcomes or trade policies that distort markets. Regular inter-ministerial coordination and joint budgeting enhance consistency and resource optimization.

At the international level, coherence between national policies and global commitments strengthens accountability. Aligning national targets with frameworks such as the Sustainable Development Goals and the Paris Agreement ensures that domestic efforts contribute to shared global objectives. Donor alignment with national strategies prevents duplication of initiatives and improves aid effectiveness. Transparent reporting through global mechanisms, including the Voluntary National Reviews, reinforces mutual accountability among countries and partners.

Public participation and open data contribute to stronger accountability and coherence. Access to information empowers citizens and stakeholders to monitor policy implementation and advocate for equitable outcomes. Inclusive governance that values feedback from farmers, community organizations, and local governments supports continuous improvement in food security programs.

Building institutional capacity for monitoring and policy coordination enhances the ability of governments to manage complex food systems. Investing in data infrastructure, training, and analytical tools supports evidence-based policymaking. Effective accountability, monitoring, and coherence mechanisms create an enabling environment for achieving sustainable, transparent, and resilient food systems.

Chapter 6: Economic Dimensions and Sustainable Food Trade

The economic dimensions of food security encompass production, distribution, market access, and trade systems that determine how food moves from producers to consumers. Economic policies and trade dynamics influence food availability, affordability, and stability, shaping both national and global food systems. Understanding these relationships is essential for designing strategies that promote equitable growth while safeguarding sustainability.

Sustainable food trade supports the efficient allocation of resources, enhances resilience against local shortages, and connects producers to wider markets. However, trade imbalances, price volatility, and market concentration can exacerbate inequalities and undermine food access in vulnerable regions. Integrating sustainability principles into trade policies ensures that economic efficiency aligns with environmental protection and social equity.

This chapter examines the economic underpinnings of food security, focusing on the role of markets, trade policies, and financial systems in shaping sustainable food systems that balance economic competitiveness with long-term resilience and inclusivity.

Global Food Markets and Trade Dynamics

Global food markets and trade dynamics shape how food is produced, distributed, and consumed across regions. Trade enables countries to access commodities that they cannot produce domestically and allows surplus producers to export to markets where demand is higher. These exchanges contribute to food availability and price stability but also introduce vulnerabilities related to market volatility, geopolitical tensions, and supply chain disruptions.

Agricultural trade has expanded significantly over the past decades, driven by globalization, population growth, and advancements in logistics and communication technologies. International trade in food commodities links producers and consumers worldwide, facilitating efficiency through comparative advantage. However, reliance on global markets also increases exposure to price shocks caused by weather events, currency fluctuations, or policy shifts in major exporting countries. These fluctuations can have immediate consequences for food-importing nations, particularly those with limited financial reserves or strategic stockpiles.

Commodity price volatility is a central feature of global food markets. Supply and demand imbalances, speculation, and external shocks such as pandemics or conflicts can trigger sharp price movements. For low-income countries, price spikes often translate into increased food insecurity and social instability. Policy interventions such as safety nets, buffer stocks, and transparent market information systems help mitigate these effects. International organizations monitor global price trends and provide early warning systems to support timely policy responses.

Trade policies influence both national and global food security. Tariffs, export restrictions, and subsidies can distort markets and create inequities in access to food. During times of crisis, export bans or protectionist measures adopted by major suppliers can exacerbate shortages in importing countries. Promoting open and predictable trade policies is essential for maintaining the flow of agricultural goods. At the same time, countries seek to balance trade liberalization with the protection of domestic producers and the preservation of rural livelihoods.

Supply chains have become increasingly complex, involving multiple stages from production and processing to transportation and retail. This interconnectedness improves efficiency but also creates systemic risks. Disruptions in transportation, labor, or energy supply can cascade through the global food system. Building resilient supply chains through diversification of sources, infrastructure investment, and regional cooperation enhances stability and reduces dependence on single trade routes or suppliers.

The growing demand for agricultural commodities has implications for sustainability. Expanding trade in products such as soy, palm oil, and meat is linked to deforestation, biodiversity loss, and greenhouse gas emissions. Integrating environmental considerations into trade agreements and certification schemes encourages sustainable production and responsible consumption. Emerging standards for traceability and sustainability reporting promote accountability among producers and exporters.

Digitalization and technological innovation are reshaping food trade by improving transparency and efficiency. Platforms for market information, digital payment systems, and blockchain-based traceability tools enhance market access for small producers. These technologies reduce transaction costs and increase trust across global supply chains.

Global food markets are evolving within a context of shifting geopolitical and economic power. Regional trade alliances and new supply chain configurations reflect the changing balance of influence. Cooperation among nations remains essential to ensure that global trade supports equitable, resilient, and sustainable food systems.

Economic Inequality and Food Access

Economic inequality is a major determinant of disparities in food access, influencing the ability of individuals and households to secure sufficient and nutritious food. Differences in income, wealth, and employment opportunities shape dietary patterns and determine vulnerability to food insecurity. Inequality affects not only the quantity of food people can afford but also its quality, diversity, and nutritional value. Addressing economic inequality is therefore central to creating fair and resilient food systems.

Income distribution strongly influences food purchasing power. In low-income households, a significant portion of income is spent on food, leaving little flexibility to adapt to price fluctuations or supply disruptions. Rising food prices can force households to shift toward cheaper, calorie-dense foods with lower nutritional value. Economic inequality amplifies this effect, as wealthier groups maintain access to high-quality food while poorer populations face limited choices. Policies that promote fair wages, job creation, and income stability contribute to improved food access and reduced vulnerability.

Urbanization and economic transformation have created new divides in food accessibility. In urban areas, low-income populations often reside in neighborhoods with limited access to fresh and affordable foods, commonly referred to as food deserts. Reliance on processed foods from convenience stores and fast-food outlets contributes to poor dietary outcomes. In rural regions, inequality manifests through inadequate infrastructure, market access barriers, and limited employment opportunities outside of agriculture. Investments in rural development and urban food systems are necessary to address spatial disparities in food access.

Gender inequality further compounds economic barriers to food security. Women frequently earn less than men, have reduced access to productive assets, and bear disproportionate responsibility for household food preparation and caregiving. These disparities affect both household nutrition and economic resilience. Empowering women through equal access to education, land ownership, credit, and agricultural resources enhances food production and household well-being. Integrating gender-responsive policies into food security strategies strengthens overall equity.

Social protection programs play a critical role in mitigating the impacts of economic inequality on food access. Cash transfers, food subsidies, and school feeding programs provide safety nets for vulnerable populations. These interventions stabilize household consumption and prevent the long-term consequences of malnutrition. Effective targeting and transparency are essential to ensure that assistance reaches those most in need. Combining social protection with livelihood support helps beneficiaries build resilience and transition out of poverty.

Market dynamics can either alleviate or exacerbate inequality. Concentration of power within global food supply chains often disadvantages small-scale producers and consumers. Dominance by large agribusinesses can lead to price manipulation and reduced competition, limiting affordability and access. Strengthening local markets, cooperatives, and producer organizations helps redistribute economic benefits more equitably. Supporting smallholder farmers through access to finance, infrastructure, and fair trade initiatives ensures broader participation in the food economy.

Macroeconomic policies also influence food access through taxation, trade, and fiscal measures. Progressive tax systems and inclusive public spending can reduce inequality and expand access to essential goods. Stable economic environments attract investment in food production, processing, and distribution. Integrating equity considerations into economic policy design ensures that growth benefits all segments of society and that food systems contribute to both social and economic development.

Role of Trade Policies in Achieving SDG 2

Trade policies play a significant role in achieving Sustainable Development Goal 2, which aims to end hunger, achieve food security, improve nutrition, and promote sustainable agriculture. They influence the flow of agricultural products, the stability of food prices, and the accessibility of food for consumers and producers worldwide. Well-designed trade frameworks can enhance efficiency and resilience in food systems, while poorly coordinated policies can exacerbate inequality and environmental degradation.

Open and predictable trade environments support global food availability by allowing surplus production in one region to meet shortages in another. Reducing tariffs, quotas, and non-tariff barriers encourages agricultural exports and imports, facilitating market

64

access for both developed and developing countries. Transparent trade rules help prevent disruptions and stabilize prices, particularly for staple crops. However, trade liberalization must be balanced with safeguards that protect smallholder farmers and local food systems from market volatility and unfair competition.

Export restrictions and import subsidies have complex implications for food security. While some governments use export bans to secure domestic supply during crises, such measures often lead to price spikes and shortages in importing countries. Similarly, agricultural subsidies in high-income countries can distort global markets by lowering the competitiveness of producers in developing economies. Reforming these policies to align with fair trade principles and global food security objectives is essential to achieving equitable outcomes under SDG 2.

Regional trade agreements and economic partnerships provide opportunities to enhance food security through cooperation and shared standards. Streamlining customs procedures, harmonizing quality regulations, and investing in cross-border infrastructure improve the flow of food products and reduce post-harvest losses. Regional integration supports the diversification of supply chains, reducing dependency on single sources and strengthening resilience against global market disruptions.

Inclusive trade policies must consider the needs of smallholder farmers, who represent a majority of the world's agricultural producers. Simplifying export procedures, improving access to market information, and supporting compliance with international standards can increase their participation in trade. Capacity-building initiatives that provide technical assistance, credit, and logistics support enable small-scale producers to benefit from global markets.

Trade policy also intersects with sustainability and environmental goals. Expanding trade in resource-intensive products can contribute to deforestation, greenhouse gas emissions, and biodiversity loss. Incorporating environmental safeguards and sustainability criteria into trade agreements promotes responsible production and consumption. Labeling schemes, traceability systems, and sustainability certifications encourage transparency and accountability in global value chains.

Food price stability is a critical objective of trade policy. Volatile markets can undermine progress toward zero hunger by reducing affordability and increasing vulnerability. International coordination mechanisms, including information-sharing platforms and joint crisis response systems, help mitigate disruptions caused by supply shocks or speculative activity.

Aligning trade policies with SDG 2 requires policy coherence across agriculture, environment, and social sectors. Governments, international organizations, and the private sector must work together to ensure that trade supports equitable growth, environmental sustainability, and universal access to food.

Sustainable Supply Chains and Ethical Sourcing

Sustainable supply chains and ethical sourcing are essential for creating responsible food systems that balance economic viability with environmental and social integrity. These approaches ensure that food production, processing, and distribution minimize negative impacts on people and the planet while supporting fair economic opportunities across the value chain. Integrating sustainability and ethics into sourcing practices strengthens resilience, transparency, and consumer trust.

Sustainability in supply chains begins with reducing environmental footprints across all stages of production. Efficient resource management, including responsible water and energy use, waste reduction, and the adoption of low-emission technologies, helps mitigate climate and ecological impacts. Sustainable sourcing prioritizes suppliers who comply with environmental standards and adopt practices that protect ecosystems. Certification systems and sustainability standards, such as organic, fair trade, or Rainforest Alliance, provide frameworks for verifying responsible production.

Ethical sourcing extends sustainability goals by addressing labor rights, social equity, and community welfare. It requires ensuring safe working conditions, fair wages, and non-discriminatory employment practices throughout the supply chain. Producers and companies are increasingly expected to conduct due diligence on human rights and labor practices, particularly in regions where governance is weak. Supply chain transparency enables accountability and encourages adherence to international labor and human rights conventions.

Traceability systems are central to both sustainability and ethics. Digital tools, including blockchain and data management platforms, allow stakeholders to track the origin, processing, and movement of food products. This transparency helps identify risks related to environmental degradation or unethical practices and supports compliance with regulatory requirements. Enhanced traceability also empowers consumers to make informed purchasing decisions aligned with sustainability values.

Collaboration among stakeholders strengthens the transition toward sustainable and ethical supply chains. Partnerships between governments, private companies, and civil society organizations foster shared responsibility and knowledge exchange. Public-private initiatives promote the adoption of sustainability standards and support small producers in meeting certification requirements. Multilateral cooperation ensures that global value chains adhere to consistent environmental and social principles.

Inclusive sourcing strategies integrate smallholder farmers and local enterprises into global supply chains. Providing technical assistance, financing, and access to markets helps small producers improve productivity while maintaining sustainable practices. Strengthening producer cooperatives enhances bargaining power and facilitates compliance with sustainability criteria. Inclusive approaches promote equitable growth and contribute to rural development.

Consumer demand is an influential driver of ethical sourcing. Growing awareness of environmental and social issues has led to greater expectations for corporate accountability. Businesses respond by adopting sustainability reporting, reducing supply chain emissions, and disclosing sourcing policies. Transparent communication about sourcing practices builds trust and differentiates responsible companies in competitive markets.

Regulatory frameworks and international guidelines support the institutionalization of sustainable and ethical supply chains. Policies addressing deforestation, food safety, and human rights establish minimum standards for responsible sourcing. Financial incentives, such as green financing and tax benefits for sustainable practices, encourage corporate investment in sustainability. Continuous monitoring and performance evaluation ensure that supply chain practices remain aligned with global sustainability objectives and evolving societal expectations.

Ensuring Price Stability and Market Transparency

Price stability and market transparency are critical for maintaining equitable and efficient food systems. Stable food prices ensure predictability for producers and consumers, reduce volatility in global and local markets, and support long-term investment in agriculture. Transparency in market operations enhances trust, enables informed decision-making, and helps prevent speculation and manipulation that can distort prices and threaten food security.

Food prices are influenced by multiple factors, including weather conditions, input costs, energy prices, and trade policies. Volatility can arise from supply shocks such as droughts or floods, as well as demand fluctuations caused by economic instability or population growth. Stable pricing mechanisms help protect producers from income loss and consumers from sudden increases in food costs.

Governments often intervene through strategic grain reserves, minimum support prices, and targeted subsidies to stabilize markets during periods of disruption.

Market transparency ensures that information about prices, production levels, and trade flows is accessible to all participants. Transparent markets enable producers, traders, and policymakers to anticipate trends, manage risks, and respond effectively to changes in supply and demand. Information-sharing systems, such as early warning platforms and price monitoring tools, support coordinated responses to potential crises. Open data policies strengthen accountability and discourage market manipulation.

Public institutions play a central role in maintaining transparency. Ministries of agriculture, trade, and finance collect and disseminate information on crop yields, import-export balances, and input availability. National statistical systems, supported by international organizations, provide reliable data for market assessments. Collaboration between public and private sectors enhances data accuracy and promotes consistency in reporting standards.

Global monitoring mechanisms contribute to price stability by providing timely and comprehensive information. Platforms such as the Agricultural Market Information System facilitate information exchange between countries, improving global coordination and reducing uncertainty. These systems enable policymakers to identify potential bottlenecks, coordinate stock releases, and avoid unilateral measures that could destabilize markets.

Financial markets and commodity exchanges influence price formation in global food systems. While futures markets help manage price risk through hedging instruments, excessive speculation can amplify volatility. Regulatory frameworks that oversee trading activities are essential for ensuring that market behavior remains transparent and aligned with real supply-demand conditions. Measures such as position limits and disclosure requirements reduce the risk of speculative bubbles.

Infrastructure investment supports price stability by improving logistics, storage, and distribution systems. Efficient transport networks and modern storage facilities reduce post-harvest losses and seasonal price fluctuations. Strengthening local market infrastructure ensures that producers receive fair prices and consumers benefit from consistent availability.

Policy coherence is essential for maintaining stability across interconnected markets. Agricultural, trade, and energy policies must be aligned to prevent conflicting objectives. Coordination among governments, development agencies, and private actors promotes predictable market conditions. Transparent and stable food markets, supported by robust monitoring and regulation, contribute to equitable access, reduced volatility, and sustainable economic development.

Chapter 7: Innovation, Technology, and Digital Transformation

Innovation and technology are transforming food systems by reshaping how food is produced, processed, distributed, and consumed. The integration of digital tools and advanced technologies enhances efficiency, transparency, and sustainability across agricultural and food value chains. Digital transformation enables data-driven decision-making, optimizes resource use, and strengthens resilience against climate and market shocks.

Emerging technologies such as artificial intelligence, the Internet of Things, biotechnology, and blockchain are revolutionizing agricultural productivity and food governance. These tools support precision agriculture, improve traceability, and promote smarter management of natural resources. However, equitable access to innovation remains a critical challenge, particularly for smallholders and low-income regions.

This chapter explores how innovation and digital transformation are reshaping food systems globally. It examines technological trends, opportunities, and governance considerations that determine how innovation can contribute to sustainable, inclusive, and resilient food security outcomes.

Role of Digital Agriculture and Smart Technologies

Digital agriculture and smart technologies are transforming food systems by improving efficiency, productivity, and sustainability across the agricultural value chain. The integration of data-driven tools, automation, and advanced analytics enhances decision-making and resource management, helping farmers adapt to changing environmental and economic conditions. These innovations contribute to achieving global food security while reducing environmental pressures.

Precision agriculture represents a key component of digital transformation. It utilizes sensors, drones, satellite imagery, and geographic information systems to monitor soil conditions, crop health, and weather patterns. This data allows farmers to optimize input use, including water, fertilizers, and pesticides, thereby increasing yields while minimizing waste. Precision farming supports site-specific management, reducing production costs and improving environmental outcomes.

Artificial intelligence and machine learning enable predictive modeling and real-time analysis of complex agricultural systems. Algorithms process large datasets from field sensors, climate models, and market trends to generate insights on planting schedules, irrigation needs, and pest management. Predictive analytics help anticipate crop diseases, optimize harvest timing, and improve supply chain logistics. Integrating AI into farm management systems enhances efficiency and resilience.

Automation and robotics are redefining labor dynamics in agriculture. Autonomous tractors, harvesters, and drones perform tasks with high precision, reducing reliance on manual labor and mitigating labor shortages. Robotics improve consistency in planting and harvesting, particularly in large-scale and high-value crop production. These technologies also reduce occupational risks and improve productivity in environments where physical conditions are challenging.

Digital platforms and mobile technologies enhance information access for farmers, particularly in developing regions. Mobile applications provide weather forecasts, market prices, and agronomic advice, empowering smallholders to make informed decisions. Access to digital financial services, including mobile banking and insurance products, strengthens economic resilience. Online marketplaces connect producers directly with consumers, improving market transparency and reducing intermediary costs.

The Internet of Things facilitates real-time monitoring and control across agricultural operations. Networked devices collect continuous data on soil moisture, temperature, and livestock health, enabling responsive management. Integration with cloud-based systems allows for centralized data analysis and coordination across multiple farms or regions. IoT applications improve traceability and accountability throughout supply chains, enhancing food safety and quality assurance.

Challenges remain in ensuring equitable access to digital technologies. High costs, limited connectivity, and gaps in digital literacy can exclude smallholder farmers and rural communities from technological benefits. Public investment in digital infrastructure and capacity building is necessary to close these divides. Collaborative initiatives between governments, private firms, and development organizations can facilitate technology transfer and inclusive participation.

The governance of digital agriculture requires robust data protection and ethical frameworks. Managing privacy, data ownership, and cybersecurity is essential to maintaining trust and preventing misuse of information. Establishing transparent standards for data sharing and interoperability supports collaboration and innovation. As digitalization continues to reshape agriculture, aligning technology development with sustainability and equity goals remains central to achieving global food security.

Data, AI, and Predictive Analytics for Food Security

Data, artificial intelligence, and predictive analytics are reshaping the way food systems are managed, monitored, and optimized. The ability to collect, process, and analyze vast datasets enables governments, organizations, and farmers to make informed decisions that enhance productivity, efficiency, and resilience. These technologies provide early warning systems, optimize resource allocation, and support long-term planning to strengthen global and local food security.

Data serves as the foundation for informed decision-making in agriculture and food systems. Satellite imagery, remote sensing, and field-based sensors generate real-time information on weather, soil conditions, crop growth, and water availability. Integrating these datasets allows for comprehensive assessments of agricultural performance and risk. Open data platforms facilitate collaboration across institutions, ensuring that policymakers, researchers, and producers can access reliable and timely information to guide interventions.

Artificial intelligence enhances the capacity to analyze complex and dynamic datasets. Machine learning algorithms identify patterns, forecast outcomes, and improve predictive accuracy over time. In agriculture, AI applications include yield prediction, pest and disease detection, and supply chain optimization. By processing large volumes of unstructured data from multiple sources, AI provides insights that are not easily observable through traditional methods. This allows for proactive management of production risks and market fluctuations.

Predictive analytics enables the anticipation of challenges that could threaten food security. Climate modeling tools, for example, simulate the effects of temperature and precipitation changes on crop yields, helping governments and farmers prepare for potential impacts. Market forecasting tools use trade and consumption data to anticipate price trends and identify potential shortages. Predictive models also support emergency preparedness by identifying regions at risk of drought, floods, or other disruptions.

Combining AI and data-driven analytics with early warning systems strengthens resilience in food systems. Governments and humanitarian organizations use predictive tools to monitor food insecurity trends and plan interventions before crises escalate. Integrated data platforms link information on production, trade, and nutrition to support coordinated responses. These tools help allocate resources efficiently, reducing response times and improving the effectiveness of food aid and development programs.

In the private sector, AI-driven analytics optimize supply chains by predicting demand, managing logistics, and reducing waste. Retailers and distributors use these tools to balance inventory levels and minimize losses. Farmers benefit from decision-support systems that recommend optimal planting schedules, irrigation timing, and fertilizer application. Precision forecasting improves profitability while reducing environmental impacts.

Challenges associated with data management include quality, accessibility, and privacy. Inconsistent data standards and fragmented systems can limit interoperability. Ensuring that smallholder farmers and developing nations have access to digital infrastructure and analytical tools is essential for equitable participation. Data governance frameworks that protect privacy and establish ownership rights promote trust and encourage data sharing.

The integration of AI and predictive analytics into food systems requires investment in capacity building and institutional support. Training programs that enhance digital literacy among farmers, researchers, and policymakers strengthen the ability to interpret and apply analytical insights. Partnerships between governments, research institutions, and technology providers expand access to innovation, ensuring that data and AI-driven approaches contribute to sustainable and inclusive food security outcomes.

Biotechnology and Precision Agriculture

Biotechnology and precision agriculture are key innovations driving the transformation of food systems toward greater sustainability, productivity, and resilience. These technologies enable targeted interventions in crop and livestock management, reducing environmental impacts while improving yields and resource efficiency. Their combined application supports efforts to meet global food demand under conditions of climate change and resource scarcity.

Biotechnology encompasses a range of techniques used to modify living organisms for agricultural improvement. Genetic modification, gene editing, and molecular breeding enhance crop traits such as pest resistance, drought tolerance, and nutrient efficiency. These advances allow plants to perform better under variable climatic conditions and reduce dependence on chemical inputs. Modern breeding technologies also accelerate the development of new varieties, shortening the time required to respond to emerging pests, diseases, and market needs.

Genomic tools contribute to improved livestock breeding and health management. By identifying genes associated with desirable traits such as disease resistance, feed conversion, and reproductive performance, biotechnology enhances productivity and animal welfare. Advances in vaccine development and diagnostic technologies further support livestock health and biosecurity. These innovations reduce losses and improve the sustainability of animal-based food production systems.

Precision agriculture complements biotechnology by applying data-driven tools and automation to optimize field management. Using sensors, satellite imagery, and GPS-guided machinery, farmers can monitor soil conditions, moisture levels, and crop health in real time. This approach enables variable-rate application of fertilizers, water, and pesticides, ensuring that inputs are used efficiently and only where needed. Precision agriculture reduces waste, lowers costs, and minimizes environmental degradation.

The integration of biotechnology with precision agriculture allows for highly adaptive management systems. Data collected through precision tools can inform breeding programs and genetic research, while biotechnological innovations can enhance crop varieties suited to precision management practices. For example, crops engineered for drought tolerance can be paired with precision irrigation systems to maximize water efficiency. These synergies create more resilient and productive agroecosystems.

Biotechnology also contributes to food quality and nutritional enhancement. Biofortification increases the micronutrient content of staple crops such as rice, maize, and wheat, addressing deficiencies in vulnerable populations. Improved food processing techniques derived from biotechnology extend shelf life and reduce post-harvest losses. Advances in fermentation and cellular agriculture are expanding alternatives to traditional animal products, offering new pathways toward sustainable protein production.

Challenges to the adoption of biotechnology and precision agriculture include regulatory complexity, cost barriers, and public perception. Clear governance frameworks and transparent communication about safety and benefits are essential for building public confidence. Ensuring equitable access to technology and protecting smallholder farmers from exclusion in digital and biotechnological transitions remain key policy priorities.

Investment in research, infrastructure, and capacity building is critical to realizing the potential of these technologies. Partnerships among governments, research institutions, and the private sector promote innovation and facilitate knowledge transfer. Integrating biotechnology and precision agriculture within sustainable development strategies enhances agricultural performance while reducing pressure on natural resources.

Innovation Ecosystems and Knowledge Transfer

Innovation ecosystems and knowledge transfer are essential for accelerating progress toward sustainable and resilient food systems. They bring together diverse actors—governments, research institutions, private enterprises, and communities—to develop, share, and scale up solutions that enhance food security. Effective ecosystems enable the exchange of expertise, technology, and practices, fostering an environment where innovation can thrive and be applied in context-specific ways.

An innovation ecosystem functions as a network that supports the creation, adaptation, and diffusion of new technologies and methods. In the context of food security, these networks link agricultural research organizations, universities, startups, and policymakers to promote coordinated innovation. The ecosystem model encourages collaboration rather than competition, emphasizing collective problem-solving and long-term sustainability. It enables stakeholders to identify gaps, align objectives, and pool resources for greater impact.

Knowledge transfer ensures that scientific advancements and technical innovations reach the people who need them most, including farmers, extension workers, and local communities. Mechanisms such as training programs, demonstration farms, and participatory research facilitate learning and adaptation. Agricultural extension services play a crucial role by translating complex scientific information into practical recommendations. Strengthening these services enhances farmers' ability to adopt and maintain innovative practices.

Public-private partnerships are central to building dynamic innovation ecosystems. Governments and international organizations provide policy frameworks and funding, while private companies contribute technological expertise and investment. Collaborative research initiatives between academia and industry accelerate the development of new agricultural technologies, including improved seeds, digital tools, and sustainable production methods. These partnerships also help bridge the gap between research and commercialization, ensuring that innovations are accessible and affordable.

Digital platforms have expanded the reach of knowledge transfer by enabling real-time communication and data sharing. Online learning systems, mobile applications, and open-access databases provide farmers and researchers with access to the latest information on best practices and technologies. Crowdsourced innovation platforms connect stakeholders across borders, fostering global collaboration on emerging food security challenges. Integrating digital tools into agricultural knowledge systems enhances inclusivity and reduces barriers to participation.

Local and traditional knowledge form a critical component of innovation ecosystems. Indigenous practices related to soil conservation, water management, and crop diversity often align with sustainability principles. Integrating traditional knowledge with scientific research creates more adaptive and culturally appropriate solutions. Recognizing and valuing local expertise strengthens community engagement and ensures that innovation respects cultural and ecological diversity.

Policy frameworks that encourage innovation and knowledge sharing are vital for ecosystem development. Governments can promote collaboration by providing incentives for research partnerships, protecting intellectual property rights, and facilitating access to financing. Investments in education and training create skilled professionals capable of driving innovation across sectors. Policies that support open science and data transparency encourage widespread participation and continuous improvement.

International cooperation enhances knowledge transfer by linking global research networks and regional innovation hubs. Collaborative programs supported by multilateral organizations foster capacity building in developing countries and enable the dissemination of technologies tailored to local conditions. Sustained investment in innovation ecosystems ensures that scientific and technical progress contributes effectively to global food security and sustainable development.

Ethical, Equity, and Governance Considerations in Technology Use

The rapid expansion of technology in agriculture and food systems brings significant ethical, equity, and governance considerations. While technological innovation can improve efficiency, productivity, and resilience, it also raises questions about access, privacy, fairness, and accountability. Addressing these concerns is critical to ensuring that the benefits of technological progress are distributed equitably and that food systems remain transparent and inclusive.

Ethical considerations in technology use focus on ensuring that innovation aligns with human welfare and environmental integrity. Technologies such as artificial intelligence, biotechnology, and digital data platforms must be developed and deployed responsibly to avoid harm. Issues of consent, privacy, and data ownership are particularly relevant as the collection of agricultural and personal data increases. Establishing clear ethical standards and regulatory oversight ensures that technology serves societal goals rather than exacerbating existing inequalities.

Equity in technology access is central to sustainable development. Disparities in digital infrastructure, technical capacity, and financial resources often determine who benefits from innovation. Smallholder farmers and marginalized communities may face barriers to adopting new technologies due to cost, connectivity, or limited technical support. Bridging these divides requires targeted investment in infrastructure, education, and capacity building. Policies that promote affordable access and inclusive innovation ensure that technological progress contributes to social justice and economic opportunity.

Gender equality is another key dimension of equity in technology use. Women play a vital role in food production yet frequently lack access to tools, training, and decision-making processes. Inclusive design and gender-sensitive approaches in technology development help ensure that innovations meet the needs of women farmers and entrepreneurs. Supporting women's participation in technology governance and leadership strengthens diversity and enhances the relevance of solutions across contexts.

Governance frameworks guide the responsible use of technology by setting standards, enforcing regulations, and facilitating cooperation among stakeholders. Effective governance requires coordination between public institutions, private enterprises, and civil society. Transparent rules governing data collection, intellectual property, and market competition prevent misuse and encourage accountability. International collaboration helps harmonize standards across borders, supporting fairness in global technology markets and preventing regulatory fragmentation.

Ethical governance also involves balancing innovation with precaution. While technological progress can drive rapid transformation, it can also create unintended environmental and social consequences. Risk assessments and public consultations help evaluate potential impacts before widespread adoption. Adaptive governance models that integrate monitoring and feedback mechanisms allow institutions to respond effectively to emerging challenges.

Public engagement strengthens legitimacy in technology governance. Participatory decision-making processes ensure that diverse perspectives are considered in shaping technological policies. Including farmers, consumers, researchers, and advocacy groups in consultations fosters transparency and trust. Communication strategies that clearly convey the benefits and risks of technology use promote informed participation and societal acceptance.

Building global governance structures that reflect fairness, accountability, and inclusivity is essential for managing technological transformation in food systems. Collaboration among nations, guided by shared ethical principles, ensures that innovation supports sustainable development while protecting rights and promoting equity across all levels of society.

Chapter 8: Environmental Sustainability and Resource Management

Environmental sustainability and resource management are fundamental to securing the long-term stability of global food systems. Agriculture and food production depend on healthy ecosystems, fertile soils, clean water, and stable climates, yet these same systems are under pressure from overexploitation, pollution, and climate change. Sustainable management of natural resources is essential to balance food production needs with the protection of environmental integrity.

Integrating environmental considerations into food system planning ensures that productivity gains do not come at the expense of ecological resilience. Sustainable practices such as efficient water use, soil restoration, biodiversity conservation, and circular resource flows reduce environmental degradation and enhance adaptive capacity. These approaches contribute to both food security and ecosystem health.

This chapter examines the relationship between environmental sustainability and food systems, focusing on strategies for managing land, water, and biodiversity in ways that promote resilience, equity, and long-term ecological balance.

Sustainable Water and Land Use

Sustainable water and land use are central to ensuring long-term food security and environmental stability. The increasing demand for food, coupled with climate change and population growth, places significant pressure on natural resources. Managing water and land efficiently and equitably supports resilient agricultural systems, preserves ecosystems, and maintains the productivity needed to meet global food needs.

Agriculture is the largest consumer of freshwater resources worldwide, accounting for the majority of global withdrawals. Inefficient irrigation practices and poor water management contribute to resource depletion, soil salinization, and declining water quality. Transitioning to sustainable water use involves improving irrigation efficiency through technologies such as drip and sprinkler systems, adopting water reuse strategies, and implementing integrated watershed management. These approaches balance agricultural needs with ecosystem conservation and the protection of freshwater supplies.

Land degradation poses a major threat to food production and environmental health. Unsustainable agricultural practices, deforestation, and overgrazing reduce soil fertility and increase erosion. Sustainable land management practices—such as conservation tillage, crop rotation, and agroforestry—help maintain soil structure, enhance organic matter, and prevent erosion. Restoring degraded lands through reforestation, vegetation cover, and soil rehabilitation programs improves productivity and biodiversity.

Integrated approaches to land and water management recognize the interdependence of these resources. Watershed-based planning aligns agricultural development with hydrological systems, ensuring that land-use decisions consider downstream effects on water quality and availability. Practices that enhance soil moisture retention, such as mulching and terracing, reduce the need for irrigation and improve resilience to drought. Coordination among sectors— agriculture, forestry, and water management—ensures that resource use remains balanced and sustainable.

Climate change intensifies the need for sustainable water and land use. Altered rainfall patterns, prolonged droughts, and extreme weather events disrupt agricultural systems and water availability. Adaptation strategies include diversifying crop types, improving soil carbon storage, and investing in climate-resilient infrastructure. Efficient land-use planning that integrates climate risk assessments reduces vulnerability and enhances long-term sustainability.

Water governance frameworks are essential to balance competing demands among agriculture, industry, and domestic use. Policies promoting equitable water allocation, pricing mechanisms that encourage conservation, and investment in infrastructure for storage and distribution support efficient resource use. Community-based water management strengthens local participation and accountability, ensuring that policies reflect regional priorities and conditions.

Land tenure security is critical for encouraging sustainable practices. Farmers who have stable access to land are more likely to invest in soil conservation, tree planting, and irrigation improvements. Legal frameworks that protect land rights, particularly for women and smallholders, contribute to sustainable land stewardship and equitable resource distribution.

Technological innovation enhances sustainable resource management. Remote sensing, geographic information systems, and data analytics support real-time monitoring of land use and water consumption. These tools inform planning, detect degradation early, and optimize resource allocation. Integrating technology with participatory governance ensures that decisions are data-driven and inclusive, supporting the sustainable use of water and land for future generations.

Biodiversity and Ecosystem Services in Food Production

Biodiversity and ecosystem services are fundamental to sustainable food production and global food security. They support the ecological processes that underpin agriculture, including soil fertility, pollination, pest control, and water regulation. Maintaining biological diversity ensures that food systems remain resilient to environmental stress, pests, and diseases while sustaining productivity over the long term.

Biodiversity contributes to agricultural stability by providing genetic variation in crops and livestock. This diversity allows species to adapt to changing climatic and environmental conditions, reducing vulnerability to shocks. Traditional and indigenous crop varieties often possess traits such as drought tolerance, pest resistance, or nutrient efficiency, which are critical for resilience. Conserving genetic resources in seed banks, gene repositories, and in situ conservation sites helps preserve these valuable traits for future breeding and innovation.

Ecosystem services derived from biodiversity directly support agricultural productivity. Pollinators, such as bees, butterflies, and other insects, are essential for the reproduction of many crops, enhancing yields and quality. Natural pest control provided by predators and parasitoids reduces dependence on chemical pesticides, minimizing costs and environmental harm. Microorganisms in soils facilitate nutrient cycling and organic matter decomposition, maintaining soil fertility and structure. These processes sustain ecosystem balance and agricultural output.

Sustainable land-use practices help protect biodiversity and maintain ecosystem functions. Integrating agroforestry, crop rotation, and intercropping into agricultural systems enhances habitat diversity and improves resource use efficiency. Buffer zones, hedgerows, and wetlands serve as ecological corridors, supporting wildlife movement and connectivity. Reducing chemical inputs and adopting integrated pest management protect non-target species and preserve ecosystem integrity.

The loss of biodiversity poses serious risks to food security. Habitat destruction, pollution, overexploitation, and monocropping reduce ecosystem capacity to regenerate and provide essential services. The simplification of landscapes makes food systems more vulnerable to pests, diseases, and climate variability. Protecting natural habitats within agricultural landscapes mitigates these risks and promotes long-term sustainability.

Water systems depend on healthy ecosystems to regulate flows and maintain quality. Forests, wetlands, and grasslands filter pollutants, store water, and prevent erosion. Conserving these ecosystems enhances resilience against floods and droughts, ensuring reliable water supply for agriculture. Integrating watershed management into agricultural planning supports both food production and biodiversity protection.

Policy frameworks that promote biodiversity conservation and ecosystem restoration strengthen the sustainability of food production. Incentive mechanisms such as payments for ecosystem services, biodiversity-friendly certification, and conservation subsidies encourage sustainable land management. International agreements, including the Convention on Biological Diversity, provide a foundation for coordinated global action.

Scientific research and monitoring improve understanding of the links between biodiversity and food systems. Collaborative efforts among governments, farmers, and research institutions promote adaptive management based on ecological principles. Protecting biodiversity within agricultural landscapes not only safeguards ecological integrity but also ensures the continued provision of ecosystem services vital to feeding a growing global population.

Circular Economy in Food Systems

The circular economy in food systems focuses on minimizing waste, optimizing resource use, and regenerating natural systems. It seeks to redesign production and consumption processes so that materials, nutrients, and energy are reused and recycled within the system. By closing resource loops, circular food systems reduce environmental impacts, enhance resilience, and contribute to sustainable food security.

A circular approach begins with sustainable production practices that prioritize resource efficiency. Farmers can reduce input waste by using precision agriculture, improving soil health, and adopting regenerative practices that enhance nutrient cycling. Organic matter from crop residues and livestock manure can be converted into compost or biofertilizers, reducing dependence on synthetic fertilizers and improving soil fertility. Integrating crop and livestock systems creates synergies that maximize productivity while minimizing waste.

Food processing and manufacturing play a critical role in advancing circularity. Industries can minimize losses by repurposing by-products, improving packaging efficiency, and using renewable energy. Technologies that convert agricultural residues into animal feed, bioenergy, or bioplastics extend the life cycle of materials and reduce waste sent to landfills. Industrial symbiosis, where the waste of one process becomes the input of another, supports more efficient resource use across sectors.

Reducing food loss and waste throughout the supply chain is central to circular food systems. Significant quantities of food are lost during harvesting, storage, transport, and distribution due to inadequate infrastructure and poor handling. Investments in storage facilities, cold chains, and logistics can prevent spoilage and extend shelf life. At the consumer level, awareness campaigns and improved labeling systems encourage responsible consumption and reduce food waste in households and retail markets.

Circularity extends beyond production and consumption to include waste recovery and recycling. Organic waste can be processed through composting or anaerobic digestion to produce energy and nutrient-rich soil amendments. These processes return valuable resources to the agricultural system, reducing emissions and improving sustainability. Innovations in waste management, including decentralized biogas systems and urban composting programs, link cities and rural areas in mutually beneficial resource flows.

Water use efficiency is another component of circular food systems. Wastewater from food processing can be treated and reused for irrigation or industrial applications, reducing pressure on freshwater resources. Technologies for water recycling and nutrient recovery help close loops in both agricultural and urban systems. Integrated water management ensures that water remains a renewable and circular resource within food production.

The transition to a circular food economy requires supportive policies and incentives. Governments can promote sustainable practices through regulations, subsidies, and standards that encourage waste reduction and resource recovery. Fiscal instruments such as tax incentives for recycling technologies or penalties for food waste create economic motivation for circular behavior. Collaboration between public and private sectors accelerates innovation and investment in circular infrastructure.

Consumer engagement and education are vital for achieving a circular food system. Encouraging dietary shifts toward sustainable and minimally processed foods, reducing overconsumption, and supporting local food networks reinforce circular principles. Digital platforms that connect producers, retailers, and consumers facilitate the redistribution of surplus food and promote transparency across the supply chain. Integrating circular economy principles into food systems strengthens environmental sustainability and enhances long-term food resilience.

Reducing Food Waste Across the Value Chain

Reducing food waste across the value chain is a critical strategy for achieving food security and sustainability. Food is lost or wasted at every stage of production, processing, distribution, retail, and consumption, leading to inefficiencies that strain resources and increase greenhouse gas emissions. Addressing these losses requires coordinated action among producers, businesses, policymakers, and consumers to improve efficiency and promote responsible consumption.

At the production stage, food losses often occur due to poor harvesting practices, inadequate storage, and limited access to markets. Crops may be left unharvested because of labor shortages, cosmetic standards, or price fluctuations. Investments in better infrastructure, such as storage facilities and transportation networks, help reduce spoilage. Training farmers in post-harvest handling and quality control enhances productivity and prevents unnecessary losses in the early stages of the supply chain.

Processing and manufacturing also contribute to food waste through inefficient operations and by-product disposal. Optimizing processing systems, improving inventory management, and redesigning production lines can minimize material loss. The adoption of circular production models, where by-products are repurposed as animal feed or bioenergy, reduces waste while generating additional economic value. Innovation in packaging design extends shelf life and enhances product preservation during distribution.

During transport and distribution, inadequate logistics and temperature control systems can lead to spoilage, particularly for perishable goods. Expanding cold chain infrastructure and improving coordination among suppliers, transporters, and retailers reduce losses in transit. Digital tracking and logistics platforms enhance visibility across supply chains, enabling timely interventions when disruptions occur. Efficient distribution networks ensure that food reaches consumers while maintaining quality and safety.

Retail and food service sectors play a significant role in managing food waste. Overstocking, inaccurate demand forecasting, and strict aesthetic standards often result in discarded products. Retailers can mitigate waste by improving inventory management, adopting dynamic pricing for products nearing expiration, and donating surplus food to charities. Restaurants and cafeterias can reduce waste through portion control, menu design, and staff training on food handling. Collaboration with food redistribution organizations ensures that edible surplus food reaches those in need.

Consumer behavior is a major determinant of food waste at the household level. Over-purchasing, improper storage, and confusion about labeling contribute to significant quantities of discarded food. Public education campaigns that promote awareness of expiration dates, portion planning, and creative use of leftovers can shift behavior toward more sustainable consumption. Clear labeling standards help consumers distinguish between "use by" and "best before" dates, reducing premature disposal of safe food.

Policy and regulation support the reduction of food waste across all stages of the value chain. Governments can implement national food waste strategies, establish waste reduction targets, and promote collaboration between sectors. Economic incentives, such as tax benefits for food donations or penalties for excessive waste, encourage responsible practices. Data collection and monitoring systems provide insights into the sources and scale of waste, enabling evidence-based policymaking.

Innovation, public engagement, and cross-sector collaboration are essential for creating efficient and sustainable food systems. Reducing waste throughout the value chain not only conserves natural resources but also improves food availability and contributes to climate mitigation objectives.

Balancing Resource Efficiency and Ecological Limits

Balancing resource efficiency and ecological limits is essential for maintaining food system sustainability. Efficient use of natural resources supports economic productivity, while respecting ecological boundaries ensures that ecosystems remain capable of regeneration. Achieving this balance requires optimizing agricultural practices, managing consumption, and preserving the integrity of natural systems that sustain food production.

Resource efficiency focuses on maximizing the productivity of land, water, and energy while minimizing waste and pollution. In agriculture, this involves using technologies and management strategies that enhance yields per unit of input. Techniques such as precision farming, improved irrigation, and nutrient management increase efficiency and reduce resource depletion. Efficiency also extends to supply chains, where improved logistics and processing reduce losses and energy use.

Ecological limits define the environmental thresholds within which human activities must operate to maintain ecosystem stability. Exceeding these limits leads to degradation of soil, water, and biodiversity, which undermines the long-term viability of food production. Sustainable agriculture integrates ecosystem-based management, maintaining soil health, water quality, and habitat diversity. Recognizing that natural resources are finite ensures that economic efficiency does not come at the cost of environmental resilience.

Water and soil conservation are central to balancing efficiency with ecological integrity. Efficient irrigation reduces water use, but withdrawals must remain within sustainable recharge levels to prevent depletion of aquifers and rivers. Similarly, fertilizer application can improve yields but must be managed to avoid nutrient runoff and water contamination. Adopting circular approaches that recycle organic waste into biofertilizers helps close nutrient loops while maintaining ecological balance.

Energy use in food systems also requires careful management. The transition toward renewable energy sources in agriculture, processing, and distribution can reduce emissions and enhance sustainability. Energy-efficient technologies lower production costs and environmental impacts. However, renewable energy expansion must consider land use competition and ecosystem implications to ensure that solutions remain within ecological limits.

Ecosystem services provide the foundation for sustainable resource use. Pollination, pest regulation, and carbon sequestration are examples of ecological processes that support production without depleting natural resources. Maintaining these services requires preserving habitats and minimizing interventions that disrupt ecological functions. Integrating ecological accounting into agricultural planning helps measure environmental impacts and align resource use with ecosystem capacity.

Policy frameworks play a vital role in balancing resource efficiency and environmental protection. Regulations on water extraction, pesticide use, and land conversion set boundaries for sustainable production. Economic instruments such as taxes, subsidies, and payments for ecosystem services can incentivize resource-efficient and environmentally sound practices. Policy coherence across agriculture, energy, and environment sectors ensures that growth objectives align with ecological sustainability.

Innovation and knowledge exchange support the transition toward balanced food systems. Research in agroecology, renewable energy, and sustainable resource management provides evidence for scaling up best practices. Engaging local communities in resource governance promotes stewardship and ensures that ecological considerations are embedded in decision-making. Coordinated action among governments, businesses, and society is essential to harmonize resource efficiency with ecological limits.

Chapter 9: Pathways to Achieving Food Security and the SDGs

Achieving food security within the framework of the Sustainable Development Goals requires integrated and coordinated action across economic, social, and environmental dimensions. Food systems are interconnected with goals on poverty reduction, health, climate action, gender equality, and sustainable resource use. Addressing these interlinkages demands systemic approaches that align policies, investments, and innovations toward inclusive and sustainable outcomes.

Transforming food systems involves rethinking production, consumption, and governance to ensure that growth supports both human and planetary well-being. This transformation depends on fostering equitable access to resources, promoting sustainable agricultural practices, reducing food loss and waste, and strengthening resilience to climate and economic shocks.

This chapter explores the key pathways for achieving food security and advancing the SDGs, highlighting strategies that integrate sustainability, equity, and innovation to build resilient global and local food systems capable of meeting the needs of current and future generations.

Integrative Policy and Systemic Approaches

Integrative policy and systemic approaches are essential for addressing the interconnected challenges of food security, sustainability, and resource management. Food systems are complex, spanning agriculture, environment, health, trade, and social welfare. Coordinated and holistic policymaking ensures that actions in one area support rather than undermine progress in others. Systems thinking helps identify relationships, feedbacks, and trade-offs across sectors, enabling more coherent and effective interventions.

An integrative approach begins with recognizing that food security depends on multiple dimensions—availability, access, utilization, and stability. Policies must link agricultural productivity with nutrition, health, and environmental goals. For example, agricultural strategies that focus solely on yield increases may overlook soil degradation, water scarcity, or dietary diversity. Integrating food production with environmental and social objectives creates more resilient and equitable systems.

Cross-sectoral coordination is central to systemic policymaking. Ministries of agriculture, environment, health, and trade must align their objectives through shared frameworks and joint planning. Mechanisms such as inter-ministerial committees, task forces, and policy platforms support communication and collaboration. Integrating food security into national development plans ensures that agricultural, social, and environmental policies work together toward sustainable outcomes.

Systems-based analysis helps identify synergies and manage trade-offs. For instance, policies promoting bioenergy production can compete with food cultivation for land and water, while initiatives to increase irrigation efficiency may impact downstream ecosystems. A systems approach evaluates these interactions and prioritizes actions that generate co-benefits, such as climate-smart agriculture that enhances productivity while reducing emissions. Incorporating scenario planning and modeling supports adaptive policymaking under uncertainty.

Local and regional contexts are critical in applying systemic approaches. Decentralized governance structures allow for policies tailored to local needs, resource conditions, and cultural practices. Engaging local authorities, farmers, and communities ensures that interventions are context-sensitive and grounded in practical realities. Integrating traditional and scientific knowledge further enriches policymaking and fosters social acceptance.

Inclusive governance enhances policy effectiveness by involving multiple stakeholders in decision-making. Civil society organizations, private enterprises, and research institutions contribute diverse expertise and perspectives. Participatory approaches encourage transparency and accountability, strengthening public trust in policy outcomes. Multi-stakeholder dialogues facilitate innovation and the co-creation of solutions across the food system.

Data integration and monitoring systems provide the foundation for evidence-based policymaking. Linking data on production, nutrition, trade, and environment enables comprehensive analysis and informed decisions. Shared information platforms promote coordination among agencies and reduce duplication of efforts. Continuous learning and policy evaluation help adjust strategies in response to emerging challenges and new knowledge.

Financial and institutional coherence supports the implementation of integrated approaches. Aligning funding mechanisms with national priorities ensures efficient use of resources and long-term stability. International cooperation reinforces national efforts through technical assistance, capacity building, and knowledge exchange. Integrative and systemic policymaking bridges the gap between short-term goals and long-term sustainability, supporting resilient and inclusive food systems.

Financing Mechanisms for Sustainable Food Systems

Financing mechanisms for sustainable food systems enable the transition toward practices that balance productivity, equity, and environmental stewardship. Sustainable agriculture and food system transformation require long-term investment in infrastructure, innovation, and capacity building. Mobilizing financial resources from public, private, and multilateral sources ensures that funding reaches areas with the highest potential for positive economic, social, and environmental impact.

Public finance provides the foundation for supporting sustainable food initiatives. Governments allocate budgets to agricultural research, extension services, rural infrastructure, and food security programs. Public investment reduces risks for private investors by creating enabling environments through policy frameworks and regulatory stability. Subsidies and incentives can be redesigned to encourage sustainable production, such as supporting climate-resilient crops, efficient irrigation systems, and soil conservation practices. Redirecting harmful subsidies that promote overexploitation of resources toward sustainable alternatives strengthens long-term food security.

Private sector investment drives innovation and efficiency in sustainable food systems. Financial institutions, agribusinesses, and impact investors play a growing role in funding projects that integrate sustainability with profitability. Green bonds, sustainability-linked loans, and blended finance instruments attract capital for environmentally responsible agriculture. Private investment can be leveraged through risk-sharing mechanisms and guarantees that reduce barriers for investors entering emerging markets or high-risk sectors.

Blended finance combines public and private funding to support initiatives that might not otherwise attract commercial investment. Development banks and international organizations provide concessional loans, grants, or guarantees to de-risk projects and make them financially viable. Blended finance approaches are particularly effective in supporting smallholder farmers, sustainable infrastructure, and innovation in developing countries. Aligning financial instruments with sustainability standards ensures that resources are used effectively and transparently.

International financial institutions and multilateral funds play a critical role in advancing global food system transformation. Mechanisms such as the Green Climate Fund, Global Environment Facility, and International Fund for Agricultural Development channel resources to projects that promote climate resilience, biodiversity conservation, and sustainable land management. These funds often provide technical assistance and capacity building alongside financial support, enhancing project outcomes and long-term sustainability.

Microfinance and community-based financial models increase access to capital for small-scale producers and rural entrepreneurs. Cooperatives, credit unions, and savings groups provide affordable financing tailored to local needs. Digital financial platforms improve inclusion by connecting smallholders to financial services, including microloans and insurance products. Expanding access to finance at the grassroots level empowers communities to invest in productivity and resilience.

Insurance mechanisms are increasingly used to protect farmers against climate and market risks. Index-based insurance products provide payouts triggered by weather conditions or yield data, reducing losses from droughts, floods, or price fluctuations. These tools improve financial security and encourage investment in sustainable practices. Linking insurance to sustainability criteria can further incentivize climate-smart agriculture.

Transparency and accountability are vital to effective financing. Monitoring systems that track investment flows and outcomes ensure that funds align with sustainability objectives. Collaborative governance involving governments, financial institutions, and civil society promotes equitable access and efficient use of resources. By combining diverse financing mechanisms and fostering cooperation across sectors, sustainable food systems can be scaled to meet global challenges.

Private Sector Engagement and Innovation Incentives

Private sector engagement and innovation incentives are vital to transforming food systems toward sustainability, resilience, and inclusivity. The private sector drives technological advancement, investment, and market efficiency, while policy frameworks and incentives align business practices with public goals such as food security and environmental protection. Collaboration between governments, businesses, and research institutions enables the scaling of innovative solutions that improve production and distribution systems.

The private sector contributes to food system transformation through investment, supply chain development, and innovation. Agribusinesses, food companies, and startups introduce new technologies that enhance productivity, reduce waste, and improve sustainability. Private capital mobilization supports infrastructure, digital agriculture, and value chain integration, particularly in regions where public financing is limited. Public-private partnerships facilitate risk sharing and accelerate innovation, combining the technical expertise and efficiency of the private sector with the developmental objectives of the public sector.

Innovation incentives encourage companies to invest in sustainable technologies and practices. Governments can stimulate innovation through tax credits, grants, and low-interest financing for research and development. Incentive mechanisms targeting renewable energy, precision agriculture, and resource-efficient technologies reduce environmental footprints while increasing competitiveness. Intellectual property protection ensures that innovators receive fair returns on investment, fostering a culture of continuous technological advancement.

Small and medium-sized enterprises play an important role in localized innovation and market inclusivity. They create employment, promote rural development, and strengthen local food systems. Supporting these enterprises through financing, capacity building, and access to markets enhances innovation diffusion. Business incubators and accelerators focused on sustainable agriculture provide technical support and mentorship, helping startups scale their operations and attract investment.

Sustainability standards and certification systems encourage private sector accountability and align business models with environmental and social goals. Companies adopting responsible sourcing, fair trade, and low-carbon production practices strengthen consumer trust and market positioning. Supply chain transparency, supported by digital technologies, ensures that sustainability claims are verifiable and measurable. Voluntary sustainability initiatives complement government regulation by promoting corporate leadership in achieving food system transformation.

Inclusive business models integrate smallholder farmers and vulnerable groups into value chains. Contract farming, cooperative arrangements, and shared ownership models improve access to markets and technology. Ensuring fair pricing and equitable benefit distribution enhances social sustainability. Private sector engagement in capacity building and skills development strengthens workforce resilience and promotes long-term competitiveness.

Market-based mechanisms such as carbon pricing, payment for ecosystem services, and sustainability-linked loans incentivize companies to internalize environmental costs. Access to green finance and impact investment capital encourages businesses to adopt practices that contribute to climate mitigation and adaptation. Integrating environmental, social, and governance criteria into investment decisions promotes responsible corporate behavior.

Collaborative innovation ecosystems link the private sector with academia, civil society, and government institutions. Joint research initiatives, innovation hubs, and multi-stakeholder platforms accelerate technology transfer and policy alignment. These partnerships ensure that private sector engagement contributes not only to economic growth but also to the broader goals of sustainable food systems and global development.

Partnerships for Global and Local Food Resilience

Partnerships for global and local food resilience strengthen the capacity of food systems to withstand shocks, adapt to changing conditions, and ensure equitable access to nutritious food.

Collaboration across governments, international organizations, private enterprises, civil society, and research institutions is essential to address the interconnected challenges of climate change, resource scarcity, and market volatility. Effective partnerships link global strategies with local implementation, ensuring that solutions are both scalable and context-specific.

Global partnerships play a critical role in mobilizing resources and knowledge for food security and resilience. International institutions, including the United Nations agencies, development banks, and global alliances, provide coordination platforms for countries to align efforts and share expertise. These collaborations promote policy coherence, support capacity building, and channel funding toward sustainable agricultural practices and resilience-building initiatives. Global partnerships also facilitate the exchange of technology and data, enabling countries to improve forecasting, risk management, and innovation.

Regional cooperation enhances the alignment of food security strategies across borders. Neighboring countries often face similar climatic, economic, and environmental challenges that require coordinated responses. Regional organizations support joint research, trade harmonization, and the development of transboundary infrastructure for food storage and transportation. Shared early warning systems for droughts, pests, and market disruptions improve preparedness and reduce the impact of crises. Coordinated regional action enhances food availability and stability, especially in areas with high interdependence of agricultural markets.

Local partnerships are equally important in building community-based resilience. Collaboration among local governments, farmers' associations, non-governmental organizations, and private actors ensures that interventions reflect local needs and priorities. These partnerships facilitate inclusive planning processes, empower marginalized groups, and integrate traditional knowledge with scientific approaches. Strengthening local institutions enhances their ability to manage risks, adapt to environmental changes, and sustain livelihoods over the long term.

Public-private partnerships expand opportunities for innovation and investment in resilient food systems. Governments can create enabling environments for private sector engagement through clear regulations, risk-sharing mechanisms, and incentives for sustainable practices. Private enterprises contribute by investing in infrastructure, technology, and market development. Such partnerships bridge financing gaps, promote efficiency, and accelerate the adoption of climate-smart technologies. Integrating social and environmental objectives into partnership frameworks ensures that economic growth aligns with sustainability goals.

Civil society organizations and community-based groups contribute to building social resilience through advocacy, capacity development, and local action. They play a key role in monitoring policy implementation, promoting equitable access to resources, and ensuring accountability. Grassroots partnerships strengthen social networks that enhance cooperation during crises and facilitate knowledge sharing among producers and consumers. Collaborative approaches increase social cohesion and support adaptive capacity.

Knowledge partnerships link research institutions, universities, and innovation networks with policymakers and practitioners. These relationships facilitate the co-creation and dissemination of evidence-based solutions. Collaborative research programs on soil health, crop diversity, and water management contribute to long-term sustainability. Sharing data and experiences through global knowledge platforms accelerates learning and supports the replication of successful initiatives.

Integrated partnerships that connect actors at multiple levels foster coherence between global objectives and local realities. Coordinated efforts that combine financial support, technical expertise, and community participation strengthen food systems' ability to anticipate, absorb, and recover from disruptions, advancing global and local food resilience.

Future Scenarios for Food Security in 2030 and Beyond

Future scenarios for food security in 2030 and beyond are shaped by evolving demographic, economic, technological, and environmental trends. Global population growth, urbanization, and changing consumption patterns are increasing food demand, while climate change and resource constraints are intensifying pressure on production systems. The trajectory of food security will depend on how societies manage these interlinked challenges through innovation, governance, and sustainable resource use.

One possible scenario envisions a transition toward sustainable and resilient food systems supported by coordinated policy action and technological advancement. In this pathway, countries implement inclusive policies that promote climate-smart agriculture, circular economy models, and responsible consumption. Investments in renewable energy, efficient irrigation, and soil restoration enhance productivity while minimizing environmental impacts. Digital technologies, including precision farming and data-driven decision-making, optimize resource use and strengthen food value chains. International cooperation ensures equitable access to innovation and markets, supporting both smallholders and large-scale producers.

An alternative scenario reflects uneven progress, where regional disparities and governance gaps hinder global food security. Some countries successfully adopt sustainable practices, while others remain dependent on resource-intensive systems vulnerable to climate variability. Inequality in access to finance, technology, and knowledge widens the divide between food-secure and food-insecure regions. Trade disruptions, conflicts, and policy fragmentation exacerbate supply instability. This scenario underscores the importance of inclusive governance and international solidarity in addressing shared vulnerabilities.

A third scenario highlights accelerated technological transformation as the main driver of food system change. Widespread adoption of biotechnology, artificial intelligence, and automation enhances productivity and reduces losses. Controlled-environment agriculture, vertical farming, and lab-grown food become significant contributors to food supply, particularly in urban areas. However, this transformation may raise concerns about equity, ethics, and environmental impacts if regulatory and social frameworks fail to keep pace. Balancing innovation with inclusivity and ecological limits will determine the sustainability of this future.

Climate change remains a critical uncertainty influencing all future scenarios. Increasing temperatures, shifting rainfall patterns, and extreme weather events will continue to challenge agricultural productivity and food supply chains. Adaptation strategies, such as crop diversification, water-efficient technologies, and ecosystem restoration, will play a central role in maintaining resilience. Integrated management of the water-energy-food nexus becomes essential to prevent systemic risks that threaten livelihoods and ecosystems.

Food systems in 2030 and beyond will also be shaped by consumer behavior and societal values. Greater awareness of nutrition, sustainability, and animal welfare is expected to drive demand for plant-based and alternative protein sources. Shifts in dietary patterns toward healthier and more sustainable options could reduce environmental pressure and improve public health outcomes. Education, cultural engagement, and transparent information will be crucial in influencing consumer choices.

The future of food security will depend on how effectively global and local actors collaborate to integrate sustainability, resilience, and equity into policy and practice. Strategic foresight and scenario planning enable governments and organizations to anticipate risks, harness opportunities, and build adaptive food systems capable of sustaining populations in an uncertain world.

Conclusion

Food security remains one of the most critical challenges and opportunities of the twenty-first century, encompassing issues of production, access, nutrition, sustainability, and resilience. Achieving lasting food security requires systemic transformation that addresses not only agricultural productivity but also the social, economic, and environmental foundations of the global food system. As the world advances toward 2030 and beyond, the alignment of food security objectives with the Sustainable Development Goals provides a comprehensive framework for integrating equity, sustainability, and innovation into policy and practice.

The evolution of global food systems illustrates both progress and persistent inequalities. Advances in technology, infrastructure, and policy coordination have improved agricultural yields and market integration, yet hunger and malnutrition remain widespread. Climate change, biodiversity loss, and natural resource degradation continue to threaten these gains, underscoring the need for holistic approaches that balance short-term food needs with long-term ecological stability. Ensuring that all people have reliable access to nutritious food requires governance systems that recognize the interdependence of human well-being, environmental health, and economic development.

A sustainable and resilient food future depends on transitioning to agricultural systems that are adaptive, efficient, and inclusive. Climate-smart practices, regenerative agriculture, and sustainable land and water management offer pathways to maintaining productivity within planetary boundaries. Strengthening soil health, conserving biodiversity, and restoring ecosystems enhance both agricultural resilience and environmental integrity. These strategies must be supported by enabling policies, targeted investments, and equitable access to technology and knowledge.

Nutrition-sensitive approaches are central to achieving comprehensive food security. Beyond increasing food availability, there is a growing need to ensure that diets are healthy, diverse, and culturally appropriate. Addressing the double burden of undernutrition and obesity requires integrating nutrition considerations into agricultural and economic policies. Promoting sustainable diets that reflect cultural values while minimizing environmental impacts contributes to both human and planetary health.

Global and national governance systems play an essential role in coordinating action and maintaining accountability. Strengthened institutional frameworks, coherent policies, and transparent monitoring mechanisms are key to ensuring progress across all dimensions of food security. International cooperation remains vital for sharing technology, financing, and best practices, while local governance structures and community engagement ensure that solutions are grounded in local realities. Partnerships across sectors enhance the scalability and sustainability of initiatives.

The role of the private sector and innovation ecosystems is increasingly important in driving transformation. Investment in technology, digital infrastructure, and sustainable business models can reduce inefficiencies and expand opportunities for smallholders and enterprises alike. However, equitable access to innovation and responsible governance of technology must be prioritized to prevent deepening inequalities. Incentive structures that reward sustainability and ethical practices contribute to more resilient food systems.

Looking forward, the resilience of food systems will depend on foresight, adaptability, and inclusiveness. Anticipating risks through data-driven analysis, fostering adaptive policies, and promoting multi-level collaboration will determine how effectively societies respond to emerging challenges. Building food systems that ensure security, equity, and sustainability for future generations requires sustained commitment, informed decision-making, and a shared vision of a just and resilient global food future.

www.ingramcontent.com/pod-product-compliance
Lightning Source LLC
Chambersburg PA
CBHW052140270326
41930CB00012B/2959